THE
COMMON
WORD
The Undermining of the Church

SAM SOLOMON AND E AL MAQDISI

D1738643

ANM
publishers

A COMMON WORD
The Undermining of the Church

By Sam Solomon & E Al Maqdisi

ISBN: 978-0-9794929-2-1 Paperback

Published by:

ANM
publishers

Advancing Native Missions
P.O. Box 5303
Charlottesville, VA 22905
www.Adnamis.org

PUBLISHER'S NOTE: *The authors of this book have employed British usage regarding spelling and punctuation.*

CONTENTS

DEDICATION

To the converts from Islam, who are coming to Christ in rapidly escalating numbers even as we speak — to you we dedicate this treatise to your defense, and to the defense of the love of God as embodied in the person of Christ, and demonstrated on the cross. It is that unconditional and powerful love which has attracted you, and drawn you out of the bondage that is Islam, and which has given you a new identity in Christ, as those born anew of the Spirit.

Don't lose heart because of those who have trivialised that incomparable love through their acceptance of a commonality you know all too well to be a well-crafted illusion. But stand in the gap to intercede for these erring Christian leaders, while remaining steadfast in your witness to them and a watching world. Remember that you are the living proof of the true love of God, as you bear rejection and persecution yet "shine like stars in the universe, as you hold out the word of life." And, in so doing, you demonstrate your willingness to live up to the upward call of Christ to be "... a living sacrifice, holy and acceptable to God, which is your reasonable service."

ACKNOWLEDGEMENTS

Of course I wish herein to thank all the workers who spent their time without any form of remuneration, or hope of the same, in the research, verification, editing, and other production tasks which made it possible to bring this booklet into reality in such a short time — starting only in early March, and finishing in early June.

Therefore this booklet can be seen to be only a first step, and a first exposure of the tip of a very large iceberg — that being initially the exposure of the true meaning of the Common Word letter now, and throughout history. But this first step had to be taken in light of the recent historic exchange between 138 Muslim clerics and 300 Christian leaders who together accepted the common ground between Muslims and Christians as being the "love of God and love of neighbor."

I could make a long list of acknowledgements and deepest thanks from myself and my co-author — which do rightfully go to those indispensable workers, but for obvious reasons I have to depend on the fact that the Lord will reward each, though their names are not given herein. Instead, I want to keep the focus on the Name above all names to whom I give full acknowledgement for all that is good in this treatise, while accepting responsibility for any shortcomings — and that name is our Lord and Savior, Jesus Christ — the one who personifies that which is being tossed around so lightly by the authors of both of these letters — The one who, indeed, is the very embodiment of the love of God and is the source of it; and, thus, is the one through whom it is even possible to contemplate the otherwise impossible command to "love one's neighbor."

In fact, without His love shining in a dark place, I, my co-author, and other former Muslims who worked on this booklet would still be among those walking and living within the counsels of those who oppose His deity, and His work on the cross on my behalf and theirs. So I give all the glory to Him, and only pray that this rather hasty epistle will be the beginning of something which will clear His name regarding the Christian response to the Common Word, warn His global church, and draw back the remainder of the 300 who have not yet removed their names from the spurious Christian Response letter of November 2007.

A PERSONAL WORD FROM THE AUTHORS

This booklet is but a first step in clearing away the veil that covers the threat to Christianity that is hidden within the so-called invitation to dialogue represented by *A Common Word* which has sparked world-wide Christian responses during the past few months of 2008 — responses that run the gamut from a formal acceptance of this invitation, to rebukes and exhortations from Christian leaders who were not fooled by the illusory images of commonality between the Qur'an and the Bible as we see imbedded within the Muslim letter.

You may say, "Who are these authors? We've never heard of them! And, further, what do they know about Islam that the pre-eminent Christian pastors, scholars, and church leaders in America and Europe do not know?"

The short answer to these rhetorical questions is that I, and my co-author, were both indeed almost literally snatched by Christ from within the inner recesses of Islamic counsel in our home countries. Hence we are all too aware of exactly the kinds of webs that are woven there — but the love of Christ, that very love that is being trivialized even in Christendom, constrains us to take this bold action to come from relative obscurity, to both warn the Church and to be used to bring our brothers still in bondage out into the light of Christ.

However much we care to release those captives, we cannot subscribe to calling darkness light in order to free them, as those at the Yale Center for Faith and Culture's Reconciliation Project have done in their drafting of a response which fooled some 300 Christians and gained their naïve and hearty acceptance.

You may think our critique and analysis herein to be "harsh," and lacking "love," but if so, remember that "the truth" must be spoken in "love," and that "love" without "truth" fails to carry with it either the approval or the power of God. So we must warn you that in seeing the "truth" about the "Common Word" letter, you should be prepared for quite a shock, as we remove the veil from hidden things.

For only then, can one appreciate the magnitude of the danger the 300 Christian respondents have put us in as the Body of Christ, the Church, as well as endangering those former Muslims all over the world, who came to Christ the old fashioned way — not by depending on spurious truth within the Qur'an, but by simply being born again, and by taking up His cross and His identity.

Imagine yourself in their place now — the place of a former Muslim still within an Islamic country — as they have risked their lives, their families, and their entire cultural identity to follow Christ, only to hear that 300 prominent Christian leaders have made the pronouncement that indeed Islam already has the "love of God and love of neighbor," a love that they, above many other Christians, know for sure to be exclusive to the claims and person of Christ. Surely this issue is a grave one, and one that needs serious consideration.

In the name of our Savior, the Lord Jesus Christ, we implore you to consider the following text and the truths therein prayerfully before the Lord.

Respectfully, Sam Solomon and Al-Maqdisi
June 2008

PREFACE

The *Common Word* and the *Response*

On September 12, 2006, Pope Benedict XVI delivered a speech at the University of Regensburg, Germany which contained some comments on Islam that led to widespread protests by Muslims around the world.[1] On October 12, 2006, 38 top Muslim scholars and clerics, published an *Open Letter to the Pope* criticizing his stance on Islam.[2] One year later, on October 11, 2007, a larger group of 138 Muslim scholars, clerics and intellectuals sent another open letter, entitled *A Common Word Between Us and You*,[3] to Pope Benedict and the leaders of other Christian denominations. In it the Muslim scholars state,

> "...in obedience to the Holy Qur'an, we as Muslims invite Christians to come together with us on the basis of what is common to us, which is also what is most essential to our faith and practice: the Two Commandments of love."

This *Common Word* document has received many responses from individuals and institutions. The most highly-publicized response was written by a group of four academics from Yale University, entitled *Loving God and Neighbor Together*[4] and has been endorsed by over 300 Christian leaders from around the world. This document accepts the basic propositions of the *Common Word* and, in places, goes beyond them. The Yale *Response* attributes the title 'Prophet' to Mohammad

---

[1] "Muslims Condemn Pope for "insulting Prophet" by Damien McElroy, The Daily Telegraph, September 16, 2006.

[2] See www.ammanmessage.com/media/openletter/english.pdf

[3] See Appendix C (see also www.acommonword.com)

[4] See Appendix D (see also http://www.gale.edu/faith/abou-commonword.htm)

and explicitly apologizes for the Crusades — neither of which was called for in the original wording of the *Common Word*. The Yale scholars referred to the *Common Word* as 'historic' and as identifying some "core common ground between Christianity and Islam."

They state,

> "We receive the open letter as a Muslim hand of conviviality and cooperation extended to Christians worldwide. In this response we extend our own Christian hand in return, so that together with all other human beings we may live in peace and justice as we seek to love God and our neighbors."

In another area in which the response goes surprisingly beyond the *Common Word*, is the assertion by the authors of the *Response* that:

> "What is common between us lies not in something marginal, nor in something merely important to each. It lies, rather, in something absolutely central to both: love of God and love of neighbor."

Neither "common" nor "new"... and certainly no true "invitation"

Is the *Common Word* the new and historic invitation to the Church and Christendom that it is being proclaimed to be? Certainly in the *Response*, some 300 Christian scholars received it as such — before some analyzed it and exposed the smoke and mirrors of illusion employed by the writers to give the impression of a common ground that is *not* there. As the following pages show, no such common ground can be supported from the pages of the Qur'an itself. Thankfully, some signatories took note of this warning and removed their names from the Response document. Others remained resolute — still under the illusion that the *Common Word* is indeed an open door and a golden opportunity to sit and dialogue with high-level Muslim clerics over the issues dear to Christianity, in the hopes of being able to establish the differences as well as the perceived commonalities. Tragically, their understandable love for the lost and opportunity for dialogue seems to have caused them to downplay the biblical revelation which shows unequivocally that the Allah of the Qur'an cannot be our God, the God of Abraham, Isaac and Jacob.[5] These scholars seem to have forgotten that 'love' must always be wedded to 'truth'[6] — the whole truth, not just shards of truth patched together to give an illusion which this present booklet exposes the *Common Word* to be.

The *Response* does not seem to be aware that "the love of God and love of neighbor" taught in the Bible and championed by Christ, cannot be supported by even one surah in the Qur'an. Thus, though the *Common Word* appears to put forward true common ground between Islam and Christianity, and purports to be an invitation to seek even more common ground through dialogue — it is in fact a patchwork of partial Qur'anic and Biblical references designed to give an *illusion* of a commonality worthy of Shakespeare's frequent treatment of appearance and reality in which he demonstrates that "oft, things are not what they seem..."

The *Common Word* is certainly not new. It is nothing more than a 21st Century version of the call to unity and peace which Muhammad issued to Byzantium before his death in the 7th Century — a call which has resounded again and again since that time throughout history, just before the Islamic forces moved in to make good militarily their claims to the right to rule politically by divine decree. However, there is an historic aspect of the document — this is the first time in history that

---

[1] **Surah 109** *Say (O Muhammad to these Mushrikûn and Kâfirûn): "O Al-Kâfirûn (disbelievers in Allah, in His Oneness, in His Angels, in His Books, in His Messengers, in the Day of Resurrection, and in Al-Qadar, etc.)! I worship not that which you worship, nor will you worship that which I worship. And I shall not worship that which you are worshipping. Nor will you worship that which I worship. To you be your religion, and to me my religion (Islâmic Monotheism)."*

6 Ephesians 4:21 *...if indeed you have heard Him and have been taught by Him, as the truth is in Jesus...*

so many Islamic scholars from around the globe, both *Sunni* and *Shi'ite*, have participated in reiterating this 'call' or 'invitation' using (or, indeed, abusing) the Christian Scriptures to back it up.

That the *Common Word* is an invitation is indisputable, but not the one which it appears to be. It is but a 21st Century reincarnation of essentially the same wording as every challenge to the Church and Christendom since the days of Muhammad — and it is based on the same Qur'anic mandate, sura 3:64.[7] As this booklet shows, the terms which are imbedded within are a far cry from those perceived by the Christian signatories to the *Response*.

Is Islamic love the same as Christian love?

After examining Islamic sources on the issue of comparing love in Islam versus Christianity, one can easily conclude that Muslim scholars are in agreement on one key point: love in the Qur'an is very different from the love in Christianity or the Bible. As a starter, the word 'love' is interpreted by them as an emotional attachment between two persons. Hence, Allah does not 'love' in this sense. When the Qur'an says, "Allah does not love the unbelievers, "what is meant here, they say, is that Allah does not 'approve' of the unbelievers, and when Allah says, "He loves the believers," he is simply stating that he approves of their behavior. Of course this is quite different from the Christian unconditional love, and the full meaning of what is known as 'agape love' in the Bible. In Christianity, God always wants to have a relationship with us, as He created us in His own image. The ultimate expression is, of course, given in John 3:16, "For God so loved the world that he gave his one and only Son, that whoever believes in him shall not perish but have eternal life." This overall theme needs a detailed treatment. In our report, we focus more on the issue of "love of neighbor" as it is a key consideration in the *Common Word*. At best, love of neighbor in Islam is restricted to Muslims, whereas the Christian expression is universal, again, as an application of John 3:16.

How then shall we proceed?

In the final analysis what is at stake here? Is it world peace, economic well-being or personal security? We believe that although these are highly desirable outcomes, our Christian heritage tells us that there are much more foundational matters to consider. The 138 Muslim scholars are spiritually lost, not because their arguments are veiled forms of the classical Islamic *Da'wa* (in Arabic, invitation to Islam), but because they are being exposed to the truth of the Bible and yet they don't see it — they are examples of what the prophet Isaiah wrote to his people, "And He (God) said, "Go, and tell this people: 'Keep on hearing, but do not understand; keep on seeing, but do not perceive.'" (Isaiah 6:9) On the other hand, the 300 (minus a few dissenters) Christian theologians seem to be more attracted to the prize of a delusional 'peace' than by their duty to confront error with truth. The *Response* did not demonstrate at any level what Jesus would have done and said had He received the *Common Word* letter. He would have agonized over the lost Islamic Scholars and challenged them with the truth of His claims. He would surely have asked the 300 Christian leaders: *What did you do to promote my message?*

This discourse is neither complete nor definitive, but it may point us in the right direction. The conclusion section will describe that — not because we want to expand Christianity for the sake of expansion, but because we care about the souls of the 138 scholars, their salvation and the salvation of all Muslims.

Colin Dye
London, June 2008

The truth about
A COMMON WORD

THE TRUTH ABOUT A COMMON WORD

Is there a basis for a genuine Christian-Islamic dialogue?

The letter authored by some 138 Muslim Scholars, *A Common Word between Us and You* is neither 'new' nor 'common,' nor is it a true 'invitation' to true dialogue — at least not in the accepted sense of a dialogue being a meeting of two equal parties.

A *Common Word*, Islamically speaking, means a call, or an invitation to 'come to common terms' — or to 'an equitable proposition' — and is based solidly on sura 3:64,

> Say: "O people of the Scripture (Jews and Christians): Come to a word that is just between us and you, that we worship none but Allah, and that we associate no partners with Him, and that none of us shall take others as lords besides Allah. Then, if they turn away, say: 'Bear witness that we are Muslims.'"

which if read and properly analyzed from Islamic commentaries, can be seen to negate all the rhetoric the Muslim 'invitation' appears to offer.

This sura contains the *common word* proposition which was first proposed by Muhammad in the 7th Century when he invited a visiting Christian delegation from Najran to 'come to a common word,' a dialogue which rapidly escalated to his demand that they come to common terms by accepting him as the final prophet and messenger of Allah. Therefore, sura 3:64 has since been the key reference behind all dialogues and debates between Islam and Christendom to this very day. This progression can be seen historically, starting with the Najran debate during Mohammad's lifetime, through the conquest of the

Byzantine Empire two years after he died, and through all subsequent conquests of the Islamic Empire up to the gates of Vienna in 1683. In more recent times, elements of this 'common word' thinking has surfaced in various harsh proclamations by Osama Bin Laden, and, though it is currently being re-packaged in somewhat softer terms, in the current invitation letter *A Common Word Between Us and You*. But the true meaning and ultimate intent of the *Common Word* remains clear: accept Islam or face the consequences.

Most of sura 3:64 is actually quoted in the letter from the Muslim clerics to the Church, so it is sitting out there in broad daylight for all to see and heed. But although it is shamelessly out in the open, it is also veiled — that is, rendered virtually invisible to Christian readers — because the true meanings have been obscured by changing the interpretations of certain key phrases of Islamic doctrine rather than following the interpretations found in the various *tafsirs* (Islamic commentaries).

Applications of this aspect of 'veiling' the intended meaning (a doctrine known as *taqiyyah* or legitimate deception) of the text appears throughout the *Common Word*, an example of which has to do with the identity of Christ, although it is not mentioned in those terms — but rather as being in support of the 'unity' or 'oneness' of God.

For example, they give a partial reference from sura 3:64 that "we associate no partners with Him [God]," but this is explained away as reinforcing the 'unity' of the Monotheistic God, rather than referring to the correct Islamic interpretation of that phrase– that Christ is seen in their eyes as a 'partner,' and that as a consequence to accept 'other Lords' or 'partners' would be blasphemy against the oneness of God. In actuality, what we would see if we were to be able to read their *tafsirs*, is that the common word they are proposing, is in fact a denial of the Lordship of Christ,[1] His divine sonship,[2] and saviorhood,[3,A] while vali-

---

[1] **Suras 5:57; 9:31**
[2] **Suras 18:4; 2:116; 17:111; 23:91; 5:17**
[3] **Suras 4:157; 4:172; 5:17**
Endnotes (A, B, C, etc) for this chapter can be found on page 41ff

dating Muhammad first as a *bona fide* prophet of the true God, and ultimately as the final messenger of Allah.

Their arguments in sura 3:64 which deny the role and identity of Christ in the Christian scriptures are supported by other suras throughout the Qur'an. In particular, in sura 61:6 the Qur'an states that Christians have been disobedient to Christ:

> **And (remember) when Jesus, son of Mary, said: "O Children of Israel! I am the Messenger of Allah unto you confirming the Torah [which came] before me, and giving glad tidings of a Messenger to come after me, whose name shall be Ahmed (i.e., Mohammad)..."**

and in sura 7:157 that Christians have been disobedient to their own scriptures:

> **Those who follow the Messenger, the Prophet who can neither read nor write (i.e. Muhammad) whom they find written with them in the Torah and the Gospel...**

Based on these suras, Muslim scholars further reason that since the Christian scriptures, and even allegedly Christ Himself, have spoken of the coming of Muhammad as, "the messenger and the seal of the Prophets" (sura 33:40), then Christianity as a whole has 'heard' and subsequently 'rejected' Mohammad, and has removed these scriptural references of Muhammad from the Torah and the Gospel. Hence their further reasoning, that, having rejected him in this way, Christians are now legally considered apostates, and thus liable for a severe punishment according to Islamic jurisprudence (sura 3:12).

Having rejected Muhammad all Christians are legally apostates

In the light of this understanding of sura 3:64 and the supporting suras, one can go back in time to the issuance of the first 'common word' letters during Mohammad's lifetime and better understand what was happening. Having already decided the issues regarding common ground, or lack of it, in the Najran debate, it became only a matter of engaging and applying them. Therefore, in issuing the 'common word' letters to the neighboring states, Muhammad was seemingly offering an 'invitation' — or an 'equitable proposition' — but on the other hand, he was readying plans in parallel to invade, all the while justifying these next step actions by claiming to have received Qur'anic injunctions to that effect:

> Sura 9:29 Fight against those who (1) believe not in Allah, (2) nor in the Last Day, (3) nor forbid that which has been forbidden by Allah and His Messenger (4) and those who acknowledge not the religion of truth (i.e. Islam) among the people of the Scripture (Jews and Christians), until they pay the Jizyah (a tax on unbelievers, specifically designed to humiliate them) with willing submission, and feel themselves subdued.

> Sura 5:51 O ye who believe! Take not the Jews and the Christians for friends. They are friends one to another. He among you who taketh them for friends is (one) of them.

> Sura 9:5 Then when the Sacred Months have passed, then kill the Mushrikun[4] wherever you find them, and capture them and besiege them, and prepare for them each and **every ambush.**

> But if they repent and perform salat, and give Zakat, then leave their way free. Verily, Allah is Oft-Forgiving, Most Merciful.[B]

Having subdued the Christians and Jews of Arabia, Muhammad sent 'come to a common word' letters based on sura 3:64 to the neigh-

---

[4] *Mushrikun,* **or polytheists, include Jews, Christians, pagans and all other non-Muslims.**

boring Christian rulers inviting them to a so-called peace, but with a play on the words *aslim taslam*; essentially 'submit and be safe, or else face the sword' — for peace from an Islamic point of view can only be peace when all surrender to Islam [a copy of Muhammad's letter to Heraclius of Byzantium can be found in Appendix A]. This play on words is very similar to the changing of interpretations explained earlier in regard to the identity of Christ, and is based on an actual doctrine within Islam, *taqiyyah*, or 'legitimate deception' — which states that when Islam is in danger, it is acceptable and even prescribed to engage in 'necessary deceit.'

It is no surprise, therefore, to see these modern Muslim scholars following their master,[5] suggesting that the peace of the world is dependent on the Christians' response to their 'common word' invitation. This soft wording gives every appearance of meaning that these two religions must come to terms, agreeing to live side by side in order to stabilize the world situation and bring peace. And it is to that illusion, and the illusion that we have the common ground of "love of God and love of neighbor," that the 300 well-meaning Christians who signed the *Response* were drawn. But in reality sura 3:64 (as interpreted by their experts) has a different meaning for 'peace' as well. It means for Christians to submit and become Muslims or at least accept the finality of Muhammad (as the seal of the prophets).

Another note of major concern for Christians has to do with the Muslim scholars' use of Bible scripture coupled with the Qur'an and *Hadith* to draw conclusions which do not follow. One example is that in the *Common Word*, not having a Qur'anic reference for 'love of neighbor,' they coupled their use of Muhammad's words from the *Hadith* about 'love of neighbor,' with key Biblical quotations on the love (and oneness of God) and the love of neighbor. This is nothing but skilled duplicity for the following main reasons taken from Islamic jurisprudence: (a) The relationship of Muslims with non-Muslims is

---

[5] Muslims are greatly rewarded by Allah when they follow Muhammad in word and deed as closely as possible. This is referred to as the *Sunnah*.

governed by the doctrine of "Allegiance and Rejection" [in Arabic *Al Wala Wa al Baraa'*], (b) The Islamic Oneness doctrine is fundamentally different from the Christian one, (c) The obligation of *jihad* with its variants and nuances does not give the Muslim any room whatsoever in dialogues — as the goal remains that of bringing the hegemony of Islam everywhere. These topics and doctrines are elaborated upon below not only for the benefit of our readers but also to propose the basis of a truly 'equitable dialogue' with Islam and Muslims.

Doctrine of Allegiance and Rejection *(Al Wala Wa al Baraa')*

Al Wala simply means allegiance, loyalty, closeness, affinity, unity and affiliation with Muslims overtly and covertly (suras 49:10 & 8:72).[6]

Baraa' is both to renounce and to denounce, that is to reject, abhor, censure, deplore, criticize and condemn all non-Islamic customs, teachings, practices, traditions and festivals; to treat all non-Muslim heritage and lifestyle as sinful and abhorrent. It is to hate and hold enmity towards all non-Muslims generally, but particularly towards Jews and Christians. This is mandatory on every Muslim.

All Muslim scholars, without exception, state that Muslims have no choice in the necessity of enmity with the *kuffar* (nonbelievers) for it is a part of their worship to Allah, it is required and obligated by Allah just as believers are obligated to pray, fast, etc. Sheikh Dr. Nasser Bin Yaha Al Hannini makes it clear when he said that "this is not Wahabism, nor is it some kind of radical doctrine of a radical cult but it is the religion of Allah the Lord of the words."[7]

---

[6] **Sura 49:10 The believers are nothing else than brothers (in Islamic religion). So make reconciliation between your brothers, and fear Allah, that you may receive mercy.**
Sura 8:72 Verily, those who believed, and emigrated and strove hard and fought with their property and their lives in the Cause of Allah as well as those who gave (them) asylum and help, — these are allies to one another.

[7] http://www.islamway.com/?iw_s=Scholar&iw_a=articles&scholar_id=841

Muslim scholars have deduced the foundational principles of *Al Wala Wa al Baraa'* from the Qur'an and the *Sunnah*. They have summarized its main thrust as:

(a) Holding the *kuffar* (non-believers) in enmity, to prohibit loving them, displaying hostility and being disloyal to them is outlined very clearly in the Qur'an (sura 8:73).[8,C]

(b) To pledge loyalty to non-Muslims, to love them or to assist them in any way that would make non-Muslims victorious is to commit a serious crime which might even lead a Muslim out of Islam completely (sura 5:51).[9]

(c) That the basis of the hostility and the enmity towards the *kuffar* (non-believer) must be visible and not secret so that they would see it and feel it, for that would strengthen the Muslim community and weaken the *kuffar* (sura 60:4).[10]

(d) That the rejection of and enmity towards the non-Muslims is of paramount importance due to their rejection of Islam which is the most heinous of sins (suras 4:48, 3:19a, 3:85).[D]

(e) Enmity must be done and *seen* to be done, and that enmity is to last forever (sura 60:4).

---

[8] **Sura 8:73 And those who disbelieve are allies to one another, (and) if you (Muslims of the whole world collectively) do not do so (i.e. become allies, as one united block with one Khalifah — chief Muslim ruler for the whole Muslim world to make victorious Allah's Religion of Islamic Monotheism), there will be Fitnah (wars, battles, polytheism, etc.) and oppression on earth, and a great mischief and corruption (appearance of polytheism).**

[9] **Sura 5:51 O you who believe! Take not the Jews and the Christians as Auliya' (friends, protectors, helpers, etc.), they are but Auliya' to one another. And if any amongst you takes them as Auliya,' then surely he is one of them. Verily, Allah guides not those people who are the Zalimun (polytheists and wrong-doers and unjust).**

[10] **Sura 60:4 Indeed there has been an excellent example for you in Ibrahim (Abraham) and those with him, when they said to their people: "Verily, we are free from you and whatever you worship besides Allah, we have rejected you, and there has started between us and you, hostility and hatred for ever, until you believe in Allah alone."**

(f) A Muslim must never trust a non-Muslim, no matter how faithful he or she may be (suras 3:28, 4:139, 5:57, 9:28, 98:6).[E]

(g) Imitating a non-Muslim in any way (i.e. in their outfits, manner of speech etc.,) is a sign of affection towards them, for Muhammad has been reported to say "whoever imitates or identifies with a community, he is one of them."[11]

Dr. Abdul Rahman bi Abdul Khaliq sums up the Islamic position accurately in his book[12] when he says: "the only business of a Muslim is to humiliate the *kuffar* (non-believer) and make him surrender or to Islamize him thus preventing a greater corruption by undertaking a lesser one. For the reality and the root of the relationship between a Muslim and a non-Muslim is enmity and war (suras 8:39 & 9:29)."

Every *fatwa* issued regarding relationships between Muslims and non-Muslims is based on and emanates from the doctrine of *Al Wala Wa al Baraa'* and includes answers to questions such as:

✦ Explain 'taking kuffar as close friends and protectors is haraam (sinful).'

✦ Is it allowed for a Muslim woman to be friends with a non-Muslim woman... and is there a severe punishment if she does?

✦ It is well known that at present Christians are extremely hostile towards Islam. So what should our attitude be towards them? Is it permissible to curse them as we are allowed to curse the Jews?

✦ What is the ruling on the call to unite all religions?

---

[11] Musnad Ahmad vol 2/50; Abu Dau'wud section on dress 4031; Sunan Abi Dawud 3401

[12] *Regulations governing peace and reconciliation treaties with the Jews and the Muslims' position toward it.* The author is a major authoritative Egyptian-born salafi leader, now residing in Kuwait. His works are read widely and highly honored in the Islamic world.

✦ Can a Muslim celebrate a non-Muslim holiday like Thanksgiving?

✦ What does Islam say about people of other religions? Can any non-Muslim person enter paradise?

More examples of *fatwas* issued by the Islamic Council of Research and Fatwa[13] are included in Appendix B. Interestingly enough, all those *fatwas* in the appendix are from mainstream orthodox Islam and are obligatory and applicable to all Muslims. The so-called 'moderate Muslims' have yet to produce one authoritative *fatwa* that would

Islam's position regarding non-Muslims has led them to resort to violent jihad

counter those which are being stated by the traditionally accepted orthodox Muslim channels who remain the authoritative bodies for all Islamic issues the world over.

Common Ground

The 138 Muslim scholars commenced their letter by saying that the future of the world depends on the peace between Muslim and Christian. What peace are they talking about in the light of the Qur'anic injunction of *Al Wala Wa al Baraa*?

The difficulties lie not with the Christians, for Christianity is founded on peace and forgiveness; the New Testament position is stated unambiguously in Matthew 5:9, "Blessed are the peace makers for they shall be called the children of God." While its stance on war is clearly recorded in James 4:1, "Where do wars and fights come from among you? Do they not come from your desires for pleasure that war in your members?"

---

[13] http://www.islam-qa.com/index.php?ln=eng

The real problem is with Islam's position regarding non-Muslims which has led and continues to lead the Muslims to resort to violent *jihad* until the supremacy of Islam is acknowledged by all.

Obligation of *Jihad*

In Islam fighting, killing, war or violent *jihad* is an obligatory duty prescribed by Allah on all Muslims: "Fighting is prescribed unto you" or as Al-Halali & Khan accurately translates the Qur'anic text,

> '**Jihad (holy fighting in Allah's Cause) is ordained for you (Muslims) though you dislike it, and it may be that you dislike a thing which is good for you and that you like a thing which is bad for you. Allah knows but you do not know.**' (sura 2:216)

Just as *sawm* (fasting), *salat* (ritual prayers) and *zakat* (alms giving) are prescribed as divinely ordained duties for Muslims, so is *jihad* prescribed on every Muslim by Qur'anic injunction. Specifically, violent *jihad* becomes obligatory for every Muslim should the call to peace (the invitation to surrender to Islam) be rejected.[14]

Muslim scholars have written extensively on the obligation of *jihad*; explaining this requirement along with its aims and objectives, the most significant being to exalt the word of Allah, that is to spread Islam by any means — first by invitation, then by force.

There are numerous Qur'anic verses[F] and *Hadith*[G] on this — all of them commanding Muslims to engage in a violent *jihad* so that the submission of all to the religion of Allah and his directives can be achieved, be it peacefully or forcefully under compulsion.

Allah does not permit the Islamic *Ummah* (community) to seek peace with the *kuffar* (non-believers) except under two conditions:

---

[14] Sura 8:39 And fight them until there is no more Fitnah (disbelief and polytheism: i.e. worshipping others, worshipping others besides Allah) and the religion (worship) will all be for Allah Alone [in the whole of the world]. But if they cease (worshipping others besides Allah), then certainly, Allah is All-Seer of what they do.

1. That the Muslims would have humiliated and subdued the *kuffar*, having so weakened them and drained them of their strength that the *kuffar* would come seeking peace.

2. When it is expedient to control the losses of the Muslims they may resort to making a truce with the *kuffar* to ward off a greater evil. For example, the action taken by Muhammad at Khandaq ditch by negotiating a treaty with the Ghatafan tribe (who were a major ally of the Quraish) and though they were non-Muslims, Muhammad offered to pay them half of the produce of Medina in exchange for dissolving their alliance with the Quraish. In this way Muhammad weakened the Quraish, and gained the upper hand by dividing the non-Muslim ranks.

One wonders, therefore, if violent *jihad* is one of the obligatory duties in Islam, could there be any religious and legal grounds for its suspension? For this obligation was ordained and legislated not only to defend and ward off harm from the Muslims but also to make the word of Allah uppermost over all other religions and ideologies.

Regarding peace, the Qur'anic injunction is to not seek for peace with non-Muslims. Sura 47:35 says, "so be not weak and ask not for peace while you are having the upper hand."

The Scholars that are quoted in the *Common Word*, Al-Qurtubi, Al-Tabari, Ibn Kathir, Shawkani, and Wahidi state a unified position in their exposition of sura 47:35.

Al-Qurtubi states: "Do not be weary: weaken not towards your enemies seeking peace: cessation of violence and making peace, do not stop the war between you and your enemies if you are numerous and well armed for Allah has said 'seek not for peace when you are uppermost to your enemies.'"[15]

The renowned Islamic commentator Ibn Kathir says in his exposition of this verse: "so be not slack so as to cry for peace for you are the

---

[15] *Al-Jami'li Akham al Qur'an* **vol 8: p87**

uppermost and Allah is with you. This means no cessation of violence, and you are not to make peace between you and the *kuffar* (non-believers) while you are numerous both in arms and in numbers because of this He said you are uppermost or superior to your enemies even though they might have power in comparison to the Muslims."[16]

In such cases, making peace with non-believers will favor and be in the best interest of Muslims — for they will regain the upper hand.

According to the *Shari'ah*, apart from these two circumstances no exceptions can be made. Muslims are not allowed to enter into or seek peace pacts with non-Muslims even though the Muslims may be weary of war, or are fearful of large numbers of *kuffar*.[17]

Seeking peace — meaning to forsake or forgo the war or *jihad* through a lasting reconciliation or peace treaty with the *kuffar* forever — is to abrogate or abolish the ordinance of *jihad*; and that is *kufr* (an apostasy and desertion of Islam). For Allah has prescribed it as an obligatory duty for all Muslims. *Jihad* is to last until the day of resurrection. As a consequence, a Muslim is to strive with his finances and with his whole being as a *Fard al-'Ayn* and to maintain a perpetual desire within every Muslim to be a martyr, being always ready to conduct or participate in *jihad* if the Imam declares it to be *Fard al E'in*, or else he would have sinned.[18]

The authors of the *Common Word* go on to say that the basis "for this peace and under-standing already exists. It is part of the very foundational principles of both faiths: love of the One God and love of the neighbor."

The love of God and the love of one's neighbor as one's self is a Judeo-Christian teaching, and is contrary to the teaching of Islam in both letter

---

[16] *Tafsir al-Qur'an al-Azim* vol 4: p197

[17] Sura 2:249 ...how often a small group overcame a mighty host by Allah's leave...Sura 48:22–23 And if those who disbelieve fight against you, they certainly would have turned their backs, then they would have found neither a Wali (protector) nor a helper. That has been the Way of Allah already with those who passed away before. And you will not find any change in the Way of Allah.

[18] There are two kinds of obligation in Islam: *Fard al-'Ayn* is obligatory for all (like fasting and praying) with the exception of those in special circumstances, and *Fard al-Kifayah* which is voluntary, by agreement when necessary.

and spirit, for Islam clearly teaches its followers to hold enmity towards all non–Muslims, and in particular Jews and Christians. In fact, that is the most basic and fundamental part of a Muslim's worship according to the *Al Wala Wa al Baraa'* concept previously outlined. The very recitation of the first sura[19] at every prayer time is a declaration of that enmity, for it ends with a curse on the Jews and the Christians.

Nowhere is love of the non-Muslims taught, neither in the Qur'an nor in the *Hadith*; that is why the 138 Muslim authors resorted to a vague *Hadith* — which, when examined, proves to be non-inclusive and inapplicable to Jews and Christians (i.e. it is applicable only in relationships with other Muslims).

> *Nowhere in the Qur'an or in The Hadith is love of the non-Muslims taught*

If we were to do just a cursory comparison between the teachings of the Bible and of the Qur'an it would clearly establish that it is impossible to equate them or put them on an equal footing:

The Bible says:

> See that no one pays back evil for evil to anyone, but always pursue what is good for one another and for all. (1 Thessalonians 5:15)

> Rejoice with those who rejoice, weep with those who weep. Live in harmony with one another; do not be haughty but associate with the lowly. Do not be conceited. Do not repay anyone evil for evil; consider what is good before all people. (Romans 12:15-17)

[19] Sura 1:7 The Way of those on whom You have bestowed Your Grace, not (the way) of those who earned Your Anger (such as the Jews), nor of those who went astray (such as the Christians).

Whereas the Qur'an teaches the exact opposite:

> The recompense for an evil is an evil like thereof.
> (sura 42:40)

And compare the Bible teaching:

> Pursue peace with everyone, and holiness, for
> without it no one will see the Lord. (Hebrews 12:14)

> And the fruit that consists of righteousness is
> planted in peace among those who make peace.
> (James 3:18)

With the Qur'an:

> So be not weak and ask not for peace (from the
> enemies of Islam), while you are having the upper
> hand. Allah is with you, and will never decrease the
> reward of your good deeds. (sura 47:35)

Can there be any common ground between the Bible and the
Qur'an given these teachings:

> Wherever they do not receive you, as you leave
> that town, shake the dust off your feet as a testimony
> against them. (Luke 9:5)

> And fight them until there is no more Fitnah
> (disbelief and polytheism: i.e. worshipping others
> besides Allah) and the religion (worship) will all
> be for Allah Alone (in the whole of the world).
> (sura 8:39)

> Then when the Sacred Months [the 1st, 7th,
> 11th, and 12th months] of the Islamic calendar have
> passed, then kill the Mushrikun wherever you find
> them, and capture them and besiege them, and
> prepare for them each and every ambush. But if they
> repent and perform As-Salat, and give Zakat, then
> leave their way free. (sura 9:5)

Then Jesus said to him [Peter], 'Put your sword back in its place! For all who take hold of the sword will die by the sword.' (Matthew 26:52)

(Remember) when your Lord inspired the angels, 'Verily, I am with you, so keep firm those who have believed. I will cast terror into the hearts of those who have disbelieved, so strike them over the necks, and smite over all their fingers and toes.' (suras 8:12, 17, 9:14, 61:4, 8:65, 2:216)

But I say to you, do not resist the evildoer. But whoever strikes you on the right cheek, turn the other to him as well. (Matthew 5:39)

And fight in the Way of Allah those who fight you, ...And kill them wherever you find them, and turn them out from where they have turned you out. And Al-Fitnah is worse than killing. And fight not with them at Al-Masjid-al-Haram (the sanctuary at Makkah), unless they (first) fight you there. But if they attack you, then kill them. Such is the recompense of the disbelievers. (sura 2:190)

Where do the conflicts and where do the quarrels among you come from? Is it not from this, from your passions that battle inside you? (James 4:1)

Jihad (holy fighting in Allah's Cause) is ordained for you (Muslims) though you dislike it, and it may be that you dislike a thing which is good for you and that you like a thing which is bad for you. Allah knows but you do not know. (sura 2:216)

How could the basis of oneness be common between the Christian and the Muslim when the Qur'an teaches 'they have blasphemed who say Allah is the third of three' (sura 5:73)?

O people of the Scripture (Jews and Christians)! Do not exceed the limits in your religion, nor say of

> Allah aught but the truth. The Messiah 'Iesa (Jesus),
> son of Maryam (Mary), was (no more than) a
> Messenger of Allah and His Word, ("Be!" — and he
> was) which He bestowed on Maryam (Mary) and a
> spirit (Ruh) created by Him; so believe in Allah and
> His Messengers. Say not: "Three (trinity)!" Cease!
> (It is) better for you. (sura 4:171)[H]

The notable 13th Century Islamic scholar Ibn Taymiyyah said "it is known from the Islamic religion and by consensus of all Muslims whosoever desired any other religion apart from the religion of Islam or the Islamic shari'ah of Muhammad, is a *kafir*."[20]

Muhammad Abdul Wahab said in his famous treatise *The Ten Contradictions*: "whosoever does not regard a *kafir* as a *kafir* or a polytheist as a *kafir* or did not try to correct them is himself a *kafir*."

Ibn Hazm[21] says that "it has been agreed to call the Jews and the Christians *kuffar*."

Are there any among the 138 scholars who would rise up to denounce those statements of those most authoritative scholars as un-Islamic, in the light of their *Common Word* document?

Basis of Oneness

How can there be a basis of oneness between Christian and Muslim when sura 9:30 states "the Jews say: 'Uzair (Ezra) is the son of Allah, and the Christians say: Messiah is the son of Allah. That is a saying from their mouths. They imitate the saying of the disbelievers of old. Allah's Curse be on them, how they are deluded away from the truth!"

Responding to a question on unity and the validity of other religions the Fatwa council stated that there is only one religion before Allah and that is Islam as all other religions have been abrogated.

---

[20] Ibn Taymiyyah: *Majmu al-Fatwa al-Kubra* 28/257

[21] A very famous Muslim scholar and minister of Spain when it was under Muslim occupation, in his book *Merateeb al Ijma* p.

Following is an extract from that *fatwa*:[22]

The Standing Committee on Academic Research and Issuing Fatwas has examined the questions which have been submitted to it and the opinions and articles published and broadcast in the media concerning the call to unite the three religions of Islam, Judaism and Christianity.

One of the basic principles of belief on which Muslims are agreed is that there is no true religion apart from Islam. . .

One of the basic principles of belief in Islam, on which all the Muslims are agreed (ijmaa') is that there is no true religion on the face of the earth apart from Islam. It is the final religion which abrogates all religions and laws that came before it. There is no religion on earth according to which Allah is to be worshipped apart from Islam. Allah says,

"This day, I have perfected your religion for you, completed My Favor upon you, and have chosen for you Islâm as your Religion." [al-Maa'idah 5:3]

"And whoever seeks a religion other than Islâm, it will never be accepted of him, and in the Hereafter he will be one of the losers." [Aal 'Imraan 3:85]

. . .a second is that the Qur'an abrogates all books that came before it. . .

Secondly: One of the basic principles of belief in Islam is that the Book of Allah, the Holy Qur'an, is the last of the Books to be revealed from the Lord of the Worlds. It abrogates all the Books that came before it, the Tawraat, Zaboor, Injeel and others, and it is that which testifies the truth that is therein and falsifies the falsehood that is added therein

---

[22] http://www.islam-qa.com/index.php?ref=10213&ln=eng&txt (text in Appendix B)

over them. So there is no longer any revealed Book according to which Allah may be worshipped apart from the Qur'an. Allah says,

> "And We have sent down to you (O Muhammad) the Book (this Qur'an) in truth, confirming the Scripture that came before it. So judge among them by what Allah has revealed, and follow not their vain desires, diverging away from the truth that has come to you." [al-Maa'idah 5:48]

...and third, it is obligatory to believe that the Tawraat and Injeel have been altered and distorted

Thirdly: It is obligatory to believe that the Tawraat and Injeel have been abrogated by the Qur'an, and that they have been altered and distorted, with things added and taken away.

In response to a question asking if the Jews and the Christians were polytheists as well as *kuffar*[23] the Fatwa council responded by stating that the Jews and Christians are both *kuffar* (apostates) and *mushrikeen* (polytheists). They are *kuffar* because they deny the truth and reject it. And they are *mushrikeen* because they worship someone other than Allah.

Is it possible to know what common basis between the two religions is being referred to by the Muslim Scholars? What can be the common basis between Christians, whom the Qur'an calls polytheists and apostates, and the Muslim monotheists?

What common ground are the Muslim scholars referring to? Is there common ground between those who are led astray and those who are guided?

---

[23] http://www.islam-qa.com/index.php?ref=67626&ln=eng&txt (text in Appendix B)

Love of God versus obedience to Allah

According to the Bible it is possible for human beings to love the Lord God because He has revealed Himself through Jesus Christ his one and only Son (John 3:16, Romans 5:8, 1 John 4:19);[24] We love Him because He loved us first and gave himself for us.

In Islam the unknowable Allah must be surrendered to and obeyed through obedience to Muhammad (sura 4:80, 3:31, 57:28), it is those who pledge allegiance to Muhammad who have pledged allegiance to Allah Himself (sura 48:10).[25] In fact one is not a believer even though one may hold the belief in One God unless one believes also in Muhammad (sura 24:62).

Isn't the twin sentence creed "there is no god but Allah and Muhammad is his messenger," an indispensable part of the doctrine of *Tawhid* ('oneness' or 'unity')? This being the case, then where is the common ground between the Muslims and the Christians who do not believe in Muhammad's prophetic call?

Love of a Neighbor

While regarding the necessity of loving one's neighbor the Muslim scholars substantiated their deliberations by quoting several *Hadith* (narrations of Muhammad) saying that there are numerous commands in Islam that commend the necessity and the utmost importance of exhibiting love and compassion toward one's neighbor.

They claim that love of one's neighbor is an important and inseparable part of one's love of Allah and one's faith in Allah; for they tell us that in Islam there can be no true faith in Allah or piety without one's

---

[24] **John 3:16** For God so loved the world that he gave his one and only Son, that whoever believes in him shall not perish but have eternal life.

Romans 5:8 But God demonstrates His own love toward us, in that while we were still sinners, Christ died for us.

1 John 4:19 We love Him because He first loved us.

[25] **Sura 48:10** Verily, those who give Bai'a (pledge) to you (O Muhammad SAW) they are giving Bai'a (pledge) to Allah. The Hand of Allah is over their hands.

love towards one's neighbor, quoting Muhammad, 'none of you has faith until you love your neighbor with that love [which] you have for yourself.' However, empathy and sympathy for the neighbor and even formal prayers are not enough. They must be accompanied by generosity and self-sacrifice.

Kindly provide us with a Qur'anic reference for love towards the non-believing neighbor

Does that love of the neighbor which is accompanied by generosity and self sacrifice include the Jews, Christians, atheists, non-believers, polytheists and pagans? Or does the 'neighbor' referred to here in reality only mean a Muslim?

Does a Muslim's love towards non-Muslim neighbor mean that the rights and duties of that non-Muslim neighbor are equal to those of the Muslim himself?

Is this directive of a Muslim's love towards his non-Muslim neighbor compatible with the Islamic doctrine of *Al Wala Wa al Baraa*? Is this directive to love a non-Muslim neighbor clearly stated anywhere in the Qur'an?

Would the eminent Muslim scholars kindly provide us with a Qur'anic reference for this kind of love for the non-believing neighbor?

Would any of the 138 scholars issue a clear *fatwa* invalidating the *Al Wala Wa al Baraa*' verses for our present time?

Would any of the 138 scholars be able to reciprocate the apology of the 300 Christian leaders for the crusades, apologizing in the same way for the brutal Islamic invasions and conquests known as *futuhat al Islamiya*?[26]

Among the *Common Word* signatories are Dr. Al Sheikh Abdel Kudus Al Salah, and Dr. Al Sheikh Abdullah bin Mahfouz bin Biyah,

---

[26] This name has been used for all Islamic invasions and conquests, starting in 625AD and continuing right up to the 21st Century.

both Saudi scholars. Would they, in light of what they wrote and signed, petition their government for the building of churches for the Christians in Saudi Arabia as evidence of their neighborly care for those Christians in their esteemed country?

The Prophet and his neighbors

After the expulsion of the Jews of Medina by Muhammad it was his directive and ardent desire to expel the Jews and the Christians out of the Arabian Peninsula altogether, as reported by Ahmad[27] "...if I lived I would expel the Jews and the Christians from the Arabian peninsula leaving only Muslims in it"; this command being fulfilled by the second Khalifah, Umar, when he expelled the so-called 'People of the Book' in 634 A.D.

So, to which neighbors are the Muslim scholars referring? According to the *Hadith*[28] Muhammad had said that: "I have nothing to do with any Muslim who settles among the polytheists /*mushrikeen* (Jews and Christians)."

If neighborly love and harmony is part of Islamic teaching as penned by the 138 scholars, would the Islamic Council for Research and Fatwa renounce the issuing of fatwas declaring the non-Muslims — especially Christians — as unfit to be lived among?I And renounce Ibn al-Qayyim's *fatwa* declaring that for Muslims to lease their properties to Jews or Christians is one of the most detestable things they can do.[29]

How can Muslim scholars talk about love towards a non-Muslim neighbor when they are clearly commanded to hold hostility and enmity towards them? This hostility being clearly outlined and taught throughout the Qur'anic text; that the enmity of Muslims towards the *kuffar* — the People of the Book (Jews and Christians), *mushrikeen* (polytheists) and hypocrites — will last until the Hour of Resurrection and Judgement begins.

---

[27] Musnad Ahmad 210

[28] Narrated by Abu Dawud (2645) and classed as *sahih* by al-Albani in *Sahih Abi Dawud*.

[29] Ibn al-Qayyim: **Kitab Ahkam Ahl al-Dhimma** Vol 1, Beirut 1991

The proper starting point for the Christian-Islamic dialogue

If the Muslims are serious in their proposals of peaceful co-existence and neighborly conduct, then they should start with:

1. Declaring the doctrine of *Al Wala Wa al Baraa'* as irrelevant, ineffective and as void for our age.

2. Declaring all Qur'anic texts that discriminate with impunity against Christians and Jews, describing them as *kuffar*, apostates, polytheists, children of apes or swine as void and not ever to be used.

3. Discarding the apostasy law throughout the Islamic world, as faith is a personal matter.

4. Equating all religions in rights before the law, with none being regarded as superior to any.

5. Declaring the equality of all men and women and the profanity of none.

6. Establishing the equality all human beings, without religious or ethnic discrimination or differentiation.

7. Discarding the practice of *takfir*[30] against anybody, be they a Muslim or non-Muslim.

For true intentions can only be measured by tangible actions.

How then shall we proceed?

Given that the 138 Muslim scholars represent the collective mind of the Islamic world (with the exception of many active movements that are either part of Al-Qaeda or resemble it in many ways), their veiled attempt to make Islam look peaceful and good, even having elements that are allegedly common with Christianity, has in the final analysis produced a very unsatisfactory set of arguments. They want us to

---

[30] Once an Imam declares anyone *takfir*, it is for the faithful ones to ensure that person is eliminated.

believe that Islam is the model of peace, and just like Christianity, full of love of God and of man.

But we have shown that all their arguments cannot be supported by their own Islamic sources: Qur'an, *Sunnah*, *Hadith*, *Tafsir*, and *fatwa*.

One would have expected from such a powerful group, an ability to state that Islam needs to rise to meet the needs and norms of the 21st century; that the antiquated rules of the Islamic *Shari'ah* are obsolete; that many sections and suras in the Qur'an are no longer applicable; and that they advocate the emergence of a new Islam that respects all humans, even to respect a Muslim's decision to change his or her religion.

Perhaps one of the most significant phenomena in the history of Christian-Islamic relations is that after 1400 years, Muslims are realizing that the truth is found not in Islam but in Christ. Throughout history large numbers of Christians and Jews have been forced to become Muslims.

> *After 1400 years, Muslims are realizing that the truth is found not in Islam but in Jesus Christ*

Yet for the past 30 years or so a great number of Muslims have received Christ as their Lord and Savior; none of them were pressured to do so. Many of them learned Islam in the best *Madrassas* (Islamic seminaries); they knew the severe penalties awaiting them if they chose to convert and were willing to make the sacrifices — because what is at stake is the guaranteed promise of eternal salvation.

For the 138 Muslim scholars, we want to urge them to look at the life of Christ and discover the source of salvation. The Bible states in John 3:1–3:

> There was a man of the Pharisees named Nicodemus, a ruler of the Jews. This man came to Jesus by night and said to Him, 'Rabbi, we know that You are a teacher come from God; for no one can do these signs

that You do unless God is with him.' Jesus answered and said to him, 'Most assuredly, I say to you, unless one is born again, he cannot see the kingdom of God.'

It is our hope and prayer that all of these scholars will take the lead and accept Jesus Christ as their Lord and Savior, very much like the thousands, if not millions, of Muslims who have already done so.

This invitation in reality is not ours, but comes from Christ Himself who declared to all mankind, starting in the Old Testament through the prophet Isaiah, "Turn to Me and be saved..." (Isaiah 45:22). He then said during His earthly mission, "Come to Me, all who are weary and heavy-laden, and I will give you rest. Take My yoke upon you and learn from Me, for I am gentle and humble in heart, and you will find rest for your souls. For My yoke is easy and My burden is light" (Matthew 11:28–30). As He, and all of us, urge you to see the light on the occasion of His resurrection at the celebration of Easter, we will continue to pray for your minds, spirits and souls to accept Him as your Lord and Savior.

As for the 300 (less the dissenting few) Christians, our prayers are for you to take courage that there is no reason to engage in dialogue for dialogue's sake. You have a duty to bring the light of Jesus to the 138 Muslim scholars and beyond. You have the huge obligation and burden to represent Christ and to allow His truth, with His love, to be the order of the day. We urge you to withdraw your *Response* officially, and work on a truly Christian reply about which Jesus would say, "Well done."

Sam Solomon and Al-Maqdisi
March 2008

ENDNOTES

A Sura 5:72 72 Surely, they have disbelieved who say: "Allah is the Messiah ['Iesa (Jesus)], son of Maryam (Mary)." But the Messiah ['Iesa (Jesus)] said: "O Children of Israel! Worship Allah, my Lord and your Lord." Verily, whosoever sets up partners in worship with Allah, then Allah has forbidden Paradise for him, and the Fire will be his abode. And for the Zâlimûn (polytheists and wrong-doers) there are no helpers.

Sura 9:31 They (Jews and Christians) took their rabbis and their monks to be their lords besides Allah (by obeying them in things which they made lawful or unlawful according to their own desires without being ordered by Allah), and (they also took as their Lord) Messiah, son of Maryam (Mary), while they (Jews and Christians) were commanded [in the Taurât (Torah) and the Injeel (Gospel)) to worship none but One Ilâh (God — Allah) Lâ ilâha illa Huwa (none has the right to be worshipped but He). Praise and glory be to Him, (far above is He) from having the partners they associate (with Him)."

Sura 18:4 And to warn those (Jews, Christians, and pagans) who say, "Allah has begotten a son (or offspring or children)."

Sura 2:116 And they (Jews, Christians and pagans) say: Allah has begotten a son (children or offspring). Glory be to Him (Exalted be He above all that they associate with Him). Nay, to Him belongs all that is in the heavens and on earth, and all surrender with obedience (in worship) to Him.

Sura 17:111 And say: "All the praises and thanks be to Allah, Who has not begotten a son (nor an offspring), and Who has no partner in (His) Dominion, nor He is low to have a Walî (helper, protector or supporter). And magnify Him with all the magnificence, [Allahu-Akbar (Allah is the Most Great)]."

Sura 23:91 No son (or offspring or children) did Allah beget, nor is there any ilâh (god) along with Him; (if there had been many gods), behold, each god would have taken away what he had created, and some would have tried to overcome others! Glorified be Allah above all that they attribute to Him!

Sura 4:157 And because of their saying (in boast), "We killed Messiah 'Iesa (Jesus), son of Maryam (Mary), the Messenger of Allah," — but they killed him not, nor crucified him, but the resemblance of 'Iesa (Jesus) was put over another man (and they killed that man), and those who differ therein are full of doubts. They have no (certain) knowledge, and they follow nothing but conjecture. For surely; they killed him not [i.e. 'Iesa (Jesus), son of Maryam (Mary)]

Sura 4:172 The Messiah will never be proud to reject to be a slave to Allah, nor the angels who are near (to Allah). And whosoever rejects His worship and is proud, then He will gather them all together unto Himself.

Sura 5:17 Surely, in disbelief are they who say that Allah is the Messiah, son of Maryam (Mary). Say "Who then has the least power against Allah, if He were to destroy the Messiah, son of Maryam (Mary), his mother, and all those who are on the earth together?" And to Allah belongs the dominion of the heavens and the earth, and all that is between them. He creates what He wills. And Allah is Able to do all things.

B   Sura 8:39 And fight them until there is no more Fitnah (disbelief and polytheism: i.e. worshipping others besides Allah) and the religion (worship) will all be for Allah Alone [in the whole of the world]. But if they cease (worshipping others besides Allah), then certainly, Allah is All-Seer of what they do.

Sura 9:14 Fight against them so that Allah will punish them by your hands and disgrace them and give you victory over them and heal the breasts of a believing people,

Sura 60:1 O you who believe! Take not My enemies and your enemies (i.e. disbelievers and polytheists, etc.) as friends, showing affection towards them, while they have disbelieved in what has come to you of the truth (i.e. Islamic Monotheism, this Qur'an, and Muhammad, Sura 98:6 Verily, those who disbelieve (in the religion of Islam, the Qur'an and Prophet Muhammad (Peace be upon him)) from among the people of the Scripture (Jews and Christians) and Al-Mushrikun will abide in the Fire of Hell. They are the worst of creatures.

C Sura 3:28 Let not the believers Take for friends or helpers Unbelievers rather than believers: if any do that, in nothing will there be help from Allah: except by way of precaution, that ye may Guard yourselves from them. But Allah cautions you (To remember) Himself; for the final goal is to Allah.

Sura 3:118 O you who believe! Take not as (your) intimacy (advisors, consultants, protectors, helpers, friends, etc.) those outside your religion (pagans, Jews, Christians, and hypocrites) since they will not fail to do their best to corrupt you. They desire to harm you severely. Hatred has already appeared from their mouths, but what their breasts conceal is far worse. Indeed We have made plain to you the Ayat (proofs, evidences, verses) if you understand.

Sura 4:144 O you who believe! Take not for Auliya' (protectors or helpers or friends) disbelievers instead of believers. Do you wish to offer Allah a manifest proof against yourselves?

Sura 5:57 O you who believe! Take not for Auliya' (protectors and helpers) those who take your religion for a mockery and fun from among those who received the Scripture (Jews and Christians) before you, nor from among the disbelievers; and fear Allah if you indeed are true believers.

Sura 8:73 And those who disbelieve are allies to one another, (and) if you (Muslims of the whole world collectively) do not do so (i.e. become allies, as one united block with one Khalifah — chief Muslim ruler for the whole Muslim world to make victorious Allah's Religion of Islamic Monotheism), there will be Fitnah (wars, battles, polytheism, etc.) and oppression on earth, and a great mischief and corruption (appearance of polytheism).

Sura 9:23 O you who believe! Take not for Auliya' (supporters and helpers) your fathers and your brothers if they prefer disbelief to Belief. And whoever of you does so, then he is one of the Zalimun (wrong-doers, etc.).

Sura 9:24 Say: If your fathers, your sons, your brothers, your wives, your kindred, the wealth that you have gained, the commerce in which you fear a decline, and the dwellings in which you delight are dearer to you than Allah and His Messenger, and striving hard and fighting in His Cause, then wait until Allah brings about His Decision (torment). And Allah guides not the people who are Al-Fasikun (the rebellious, disobedient to Allah).

Sura 60:1 O you who believe! Take not My enemies and your enemies (i.e. disbelievers and polytheists, etc.) as friends, showing affection towards them, while they have disbelieved in what has come to you of the truth (i.e. Islamic Monotheism, this Qur'anic, and Muhammad)

D   Sura 4:48 Allah forgives not that partners should be set up with Him; but He forgives anything else, to whom He pleases; to set up partners with Allah is to devise a sin Most heinous indeed.

Sura 3:19 Truly, the religion with Allah is Islam.

Sura 3:85 And whoever seeks a religion other than Islam, it will never be accepted of him, and in the Hereafter he will be one of the losers.

E Sura 3:28 Let not the believers take the disbelievers as Auliyâ (supporters, helpers, etc.) instead of the believers, and whoever does that will never be helped by Allah in any way, except if you indeed fear a danger from them. And Allah warns you against Himself (His Punishment), and to Allah is the final return.

Sura 4:139 Those who take disbelievers for Auliyâ' (protectors or helpers or friends) instead of believers, do they seek honour, power and glory with them?

Sura 5:57 O you who believe! Take not for Auliyâ' (protectors and helpers) those who take your religion for a mockery and fun from among those who received the Scripture (Jews and Christians) before you, nor from among the disbelievers; and fear Allah if you indeed are true believers.

Sura 9:28 O you who believe in Allah's Oneness and in His Messenger! Verily, the Mushrikûn (polytheists, pagans, idolaters, disbelievers in the Oneness of Allah, and in the Message of Muhammad) are Najasun (impure). So let them not come near Al-Masjid-al-Harâm (at Makkah) after this year, and if you fear poverty, Allah will enrich you if He will, out of His Bounty.

Sura 98:6 Verily, those who disbelieve (in the religion of Islâm, the Qur'ân and Prophet Muhammad (Peace be upon him)) from among the people of the Scripture (Jews and Christians) and Al-Mushrikûn will abide in the Fire of Hell. They are the worst of creatures.

F Sura 9:33 It is Allah Who sent His Messenger (Muhammad) with guidance and the religion of truth, (Islam) that He might cause it to prevail over all religion, through the polytheists (polytheists, pagans, idolaters, disbelievers in the Oneness of Allah) may detest it.

Sura 9:29 Fight against those who (1) believe not in Allah, (2) nor in the Last Day, (3) nor forbid that which has been forbidden by Allah and His Messenger (4) and those who acknowledge not the religion of truth (i.e. Islam) among the people of the Scripture (Jews and Christians), until they pay the Jizyah with willing submission, and feel themselves subdued.

Sura 8:39 And fight them until there is no more Fitnah (disbelief and polytheism: worshipping others besides Allah and would believe in Muhammad, and the religion (worship) will all be for Allah Alone Islam <in the whole of the world>. But if they cease (worshipping others besides Allah), then certainly, Allah is All-Seer of what they do.

G It is reported by Abi Musa said that a man came to the prophet of Allah saying did you see a man fighting against strength, against a garrison, and against hypocrisy which of them is for the sake of Allah? He said the Apostle of Allah said whosoever fights to exalt the word of Allah is for the sake of Allah. Reported by Musnad Ahmad 18722, Al-Nasa'i 3085, Abu Dawud 2156, Al-Tirmidhi 1570, Al Bukhari 2599, 6904.

Reported by Ibn Umar who said that the Apostle of Allah said I have been sent for this hour with a sword in between my hands that Only Allah alone would be worshipped who has no partners, He who has made my living under my sword, and has humiliated those who would oppose my commands and whose ever imitates a people he would be one of them. Ahmed 4869, 9109.

Sura 2:193 And fight them until there is no more Fitnah (disbelief and worshipping of others along with Allah) and (all and every kind of) worship is for Allah (Alone) [meaning that they believed in Muhammad]. But if they cease, let there be no transgression except against Az-zalimun (the polytheists, and wrong-doers).

It is reported by Tamim Ad-Dari that it is as certain as the night follows day that Allah would not leave a house high or low until Allah enrolls it in this religion through an honour or humiliation, *Musnad Ahmad* 16344.

From Aunsi bin Malik that the Apostle of Allah said that I have been commanded to kill until they testify that there is no god but Allah, and Muhammad is his apostle so if they recited that there is no god but Allah and Muhammad is his apostle and accepted our Qibla (the prayer direction towards Mecca) and eat our sacrifices, and prayed our prayers, then it is forbidden to us to shed their blood, or to take their wealth, except and all their rights except what is due to them what is due to the Muslims. Ahmad 1289, Al Bukhari 6413.

From Abu Huraira from the apostle of Allah who said I have been commanded to kill/fight people until such time they recite the creed there is no god but allah and belief in me and what I have come with and if they did that they would have secured their blood, their money, properties with truth and its account is with Allah. Muslim 31, 32, 33, Ahmad 8188, Al Bukhari 24.

H Further teaching on this is found in suras 5:17, 72, and 73.

Surely, in disbelief are they who say that Allah is the Messiah, son of Maryam. Say (O Muhammad SAW): "Who then has the least power against Allah, if He were to destroy the Messiah, son of Maryam his mother, and all those who are on the earth together?" And to Allah belongs the dominion of the heavens and the earth, and all that is between them. He creates what He wills. And Allah is Able to do all things.

Surely, they have disbelieved who say: "Allah is the Messiah ['Iesa (Jesus)], son of Maryam (Mary)." Surely, disbelievers are those who said: "Allah is the third of the three (in a Trinity)." I Further fatwas are found in Appendix B.

APPENDIX A:
Heraclius of Byzantium

In 630AD Muhammad wrote to Heraclius, Emperor of Byzantium (the Hellenic Empire ruled from Constantinople), inviting him to aslim taslam or to "come to common terms." Here, in one of the earliest surviving examples of the "common word" invitation we can see the written Arabic, English translation and a facsimile of the original document.

The translated text of Muhammad's letter to Heraclius of Byzantium

> In the name of Allah the compassionate and merciful,
>
> From Muhammad, messenger of Allah, to Mighty Heraclius of Byzantinium: peace on those who followed the guidance. Hereafter, I invite you with the invitation of Islam: *aslim taslam*; surrender and be safe. If you embrace Islam Allah will double your portion, but if you refuse on you will be [committing] the sin of being Ariuseen (cultic). Sura 3:64 Say (O Muhammad): "O people of the Scripture (Jews and Christians): Come to common terms, between us and you, that we worship none but Allah, and that we associate no partners with Him, and that none of us shall take others as lords besides Allah. Then, if they turn away, say: 'Bear witness that we are Muslims.'"

APPENDIX B:
Fatwas

There have been a large number of *fatwas* issued covering various aspects of Muslim relationships with non-Muslims; a selection has been reproduced here. All the listed fatwa are in an abridged form, however the appropriate site is given should one desire to read the full version of it as given by the Muslims scholars.

Note: Whereas in the main document the authors have, as far as possible, standardized the English translation and usage of Arabic words, in this section they have followed the conventions used by the individual writers quoted.

Question: We hope that you will be able to explain, with examples, what is meant by the phrase, "Taking *kuffar* as close friends and protectors is *haraam*."

Answer: Yes, examples will certainly explain and clarify what is meant, so we will move straight on to quoting some of the most important points that the scholars and leaders of *da'wah* have said:

Muslims should not:

1. Prefer the *kuffar* to the Muslims.
2. Refer to them for judgment.
3. Be befriending and liking them.
4. Be inclining towards them, relying upon them and taking them as a support, or helping and supporting them against the Muslims.
5. Become members of their societies, join their parties, increasing their numbers, taking their nationalities (except

in cases of necessity), serving in their armies or help to develop their weapons.

6. Bringing their laws and rules to the Muslim countries.

7. Take them as friends in general terms, taking them as helpers and supporters, and throwing in one's lot with them.

8. Compromising with them and being nice to them at the expense of one's religion. This includes sitting with them and entering upon them at the time when they are making fun of the Signs of Allah.

9. Trust them and take them as advisors and consultants instead of the believers. From these texts it is clear that we are forbidden to appoint *kuffar* to positions whereby they could find out the secrets of the Muslims and plot against them by trying to do all kinds of harm.

10. Putting them in administrative positions where they are bosses of Muslims and can humiliate them, run their affairs and prevent them from practising their religion. Similarly, we should not employ them in Muslim homes where they can see our private matters and they bring our children up as *kuffar*. This is what is happening nowadays when *kuffar* are brought to Muslim countries as workers, drivers, servants and nannies in Muslim homes and families.

    Neither should we send our children to *kafir* schools, missionary institutions and evil colleges and universities, or make them live with *kafir* families.

11. Imitating the *kuffar* in dress, appearance, speech, etc., because this indicates love of the person or people imitated. The Prophet said: "Whoever imitates a people is one of them."

    It is forbidden to imitate the *kuffar* in customs, habits and matters of outward appearance and conduct that are characteristic of them. This includes shaving the beard, letting the moustache grow long, and speaking their languages, except when necessary, as well as matters of clothing, food and drink, etc.

Staying in their countries when there is no need to do so. Nobody will be excused for staying in a *kafir* country except for those who are truly weak and oppressed and cannot migrate, or those who stay among them for a valid religious purpose such as *da'wah* and spreading Islam in their countries.

It is forbidden to live among them when there is no need to do so. The Prophet said: "I disown the one who stays among the *mushrikeen*."

13. Praising them and their civilization and culture, defending them, and admiring their behavior and skills, without taking note of their false ideology and corrupt religion. Forsaking the Islamic calendar and using their calendar, especially since it reflects their rituals and festivals, as is the case with the Gregorian (Western) calendar, which is connected to the supposed date of the birth of the Messiah (peace be upon him), which is an innovation that they have fabricated and that has nothing to do with the religion of 'Eesa (Jesus). Using this calendar implies approval of their festivals and symbols.

14. Take part in their holidays and festivals, helping them to celebrate them, congratulating them on these occasions or attending places where such celebrations are held.

15. Seek forgiveness for them and asking Allah for mercy for them.

These examples should give a clear picture of what is meant by the prohibition of forming close friendships with the *kuffar*. We ask Allah to keep our belief sound and our faith strong. And Allah is the Source of Help.

Sheikh Muhammad Salih Al-Munajjid
http://www.islam-qa.com/index.php?ref=2179&ln=eng&txt

Question : Is it allowed for a Muslim woman to be friends with a non-Muslim woman who is very decent, without neglecting her one religion and is there a severe punishment if she does?

Answer: Undoubtedly making friends with a *kafir* woman will adversely affect her religious commitment, because a *kafir* woman does not behave in the same manner or have the same attitude as a Muslim woman, and she does not worship Allah according to the religion of Islam. Therefore she will not avoid doing things that may adversely affect this Muslim woman who may be deceived by the modest dress or good manners of this *kafir* woman, especially in matters that will adversely affect her religious commitment.

Similarly, making friends with her may lead to some kind of approval in one's heart for the rituals that she does as part of her own religion, and this will weaken the sense of friendship and enmity for the sake of Allah (*al-wala' wa'l-bara'*).

Indeed, it may lead some ignorant people to disapprove of the ruling of Allah that the *kuffar* are disbelievers who will abide in Hell forever — we seek refuge with Allah. Hence the Prophet said: "Do not keep company with anyone but a believer and do not let anyone eat your food but one who is pious." (Narrated by al-Tirmidhi, 2395; Abu Dawood, 4832; classed as *saheeh* by Ibn Hibbaan, 2/314; classed as *hasan* by Shaykh al-Albaani in Saheeh al-Jaami', 7341).

We do not mean, however, that this Muslim woman should cut herself off completely from the *kafir* woman; she may visit with her, visit her when she is sick and give her gifts, but without forming an emotional attachment or joining in their festivals and celebrations. And the Muslim woman should aim, in those visits and gift-giving, to call this *kafir* woman to Islam.

Shaykh Saalih al-Fawzaan said: There is nothing wrong with visiting *kuffar* in order to call them to Islam.

But visiting *kuffar* in order to have a good time with them is not permitted, because it is obligatory to hate them and shun them.

http://www.islam-qa.com/index.php?ref=23325&ln=eng&txt

Question: In His Book, Allah says of the Christians "Verily, you will find the strongest among men in enmity to the believers (Muslims) the Jews and those who are Al Mushrikoon, and you will find the nearest in love to the believers (Muslims) those who say: 'We are Christians'" [al-Maa'idah 5:82] It is well known that at present they are extremely hostile towards Islam. So what should our attitude be toward them? Is it permissible to curse them as we are allowed to curse the Jews? This issue is confusing me a great deal.

Answer: The praise mentioned in these verses should not cause any confusion regarding the Christians or make us refrain from cursing them. The description in the verses does not include all Christians, rather it refers to a group among them who responded to the truth and were not too arrogant to follow it. This is what is implied by the context of the verses asked about:

"Verily, you will find the strongest among men in enmity to the believers (Muslims) the Jews and those who are *Al-Mushrikoon*, and you will find the nearest in love to the believers (Muslims) those who say: 'We are Christians.' That is because amongst them are priests and monks, and they are not proud."

These verses are speaking of some Christian people who, when they came to know the truth, became Muslim and declared their faith.

The great scholar Ibn al-Qayyim said concerning these verses: What is meant is that the people described here, when they realized that he was the Messenger of Allah according to the description that they had, they could not stop their eyes from weeping or their hearts from hastening to believe.

With regard to cursing those among the Christians who do not believe in Muhammad, there is innumerable definitive evidence which points to that, such as the hadeeth narrated by al-Bukhaari and Muslim in their *Saheehs* from *'Aa'ishah*, which says that the Messenger of Allah said, during his final illness: "May Allah curse the Jews and Christians, for they took the graves of their Prophets as places of worship." How can they not be cursed when Allah has described them in His Book as follows:

> Surely, they have disbelieved who say: 'Allah is the Messiah ['Eesa (Jesus)], son of Maryam (Mary).' [al-Maa'idah 5:72]

> Surely, disbelievers are those who said: 'Allah is the third of the three (in a Trinity).' [al-Maa'idah 5:73]

And there are other texts which speak of their *kufr* (disbelief) and misguidance. Among the verses which speak of their ultimate destiny is the last of the verses in the passage referred to by the questioner, where Allah says (interpretation of the meaning):

> But those who disbelieved and belied Our *Ayaat* (proofs, evidences, verses, lessons, signs, revelations, etc.), they shall be the dwellers of the (Hell) Fire [al-Maa'idah 5:86]

From a *fatwa* of Shaykh Ibn Ibraaheem. Majallat al-Buhooth al-Islamiyyah, 58/36-39.

See Sheikh Abdul Rahman bi Abdul Khaliq's book on www.salafi.net on the issue of peace treaty:

The peace treaties between few of the Arab Political leaders and the Jews are futile ineffective and legally invalid from the *shari'ah* point of view. It is inappropriate for any Muslim neither to take it as valid nor to implement any part of it except what is there forcefully and of a compulsion.

The proofs that these treaties are legally invalid, ineffective and non-implementable (from *shari'ah* point of view) are:

These treaties stipulate the cessation of war between the Muslims and the Jews forever. That is an invalid proposition because the jihad that is against them is an obligation on every Muslim. It's valid and its viability decreed to be effective until the day of judgment and it can't be annulled from the laws of Allah by anyone. Whosoever believes that the *jihad* is nonexistent and attempts to nullify it, is a *kafir* and must be excommunicated as he would have denied the very core essentials of the religion.

For (violent) *jihad* is valid and effective until the day of judgment substantiated by the Qur'an, *Sunnah* and the *I'jma*. However, it's permissible that the ceasefire agreement can be drawn for few years where it's in the interest of the Muslims, without time specification.

But to state that the violent war with the Jews has ended forever and this is a comprehensive peace treaty lasting forever, is to invalidate, nullifying the ordinance of *jihad*, **making concession to the *kuffar* in their apostasy and accepting them on the basis of their *kufur*, this remains forbidden and beyond the bounds of a Muslim forever. Unless he renegades on Allah and his message.**

Secondly the treaties stipulated that the parties would do their utmost to remove the factors causing (basis/reasons behind) enmity, hostility, and all other directives of the *shari'ah* that may be fuelling such enmity.

This condition or pre-requisite is invalid because it contradicts the very nature of Islamic faith. For Islamic faith is based on the separation of Muslim and *kafir* and that the *kafir* is an enemy of Allah forever until he embraces Islam discarding his *kufur*, Allah has forbidden the believers from pleading any allegiance to the *kuffar* or showing them any affection even if they were their fathers, brothers, children or kinsmen or their spouses as stated in sura 58:22.

http://www.islam-qa.com/index.php?ref=22182&ln=eng&txt

Question : What are Ruling on the call to unite all religions?

Answer: The Standing Committee on Academic Research and Issuing Fatwas has examined the questions which have been submitted to it and the opinions and articles published and broadcast in the media concerning the call to unite the three religions of Islam, Judaism and Christianity; and the call which stems from that, to build a mosque, a church and a synagogue in one place, on university campuses and in public squares; and the call to print the Qur'an, *Tawraat* (Torah) and *Injeel* (Gospel) in one volume, etc.; and the conferences, seminars and meetings on this topic which are being held in the east and in the west. After studying and pondering the matter, the Committee issues the following statement:

One of the basic principles of belief in Islam, on which all the Muslims are agreed (*ijmaa'*) is that there is no true religion on the face of the earth apart from Islam. It is the final religion which abrogates all religions and laws that came before it. There is no religion on earth according to which Allah is to be worshipped apart from Islam. "And whoever seeks a religion other than Islâm, it will never be accepted of him, and in the Hereafter he will be one of the losers" [3:85]. After the coming of Muhammad, Islam means what he brought, not any other religion.

One of the basic principles of belief in Islam is that the Book of Allah, the Holy Qur'an, is the last of the Books to be revealed from the Lord of the Worlds. It abrogates all the Books that came before it, the *Tawraat*, *Zaboor*, *Injeel* and others. So there is no longer any revealed Book according to which Allah may be worshipped apart from the Qur'an.

It is obligatory to believe that the *Tawraat* and *Injeel* have been abrogated by the Qur'an, and that they have been altered and distorted, with things added and taken away,

"Then woe to those who write the Book with their own hands and then say, "This is from Allah,""

to purchase with it a little price! Woe to them for what their hands have written and woe to them for that they earn thereby." [*al-Baqarah* 2:79]

"And verily, among them is a party who distort the Book with their tongues (as they read), so that you may think it is from the Book, but it is not from the Book, and they say: "This is from Allah," but it is not from Allah; and they speak a lie against Allah while they know it." [*Aal 'Imraan* 3:78]

Hence, whatever in the previous books was correct is abrogated by Islam, and everything else is distorted and changed.

One of the basic principles of belief in Islam is that we must believe that every Jew, Christian or other person who does not enter Islam is a *kafir*, and that those against whom proof is established must be named as *kuffar* and regarded as enemies of Allah, His Messenger and the believers, and that they are the people of Hell.

In the light of these basic principles of belief and the rulings of *sharee'ah*, calling for the uniting of all religions, and for them to be brought close to one another and cast in the same mould, is an evil and crafty call whose aim is to mix truth with falsehood, to destroy Islam and undermine its pillars, and to tempt its followers into total apostasy.

Among the effects of this evil call would be the cancelling out of the differences between Islam and *kuffar*, truth and falsehood, good and evil. It would break down the psychological barrier that exists between the Muslims and the *kuffar*, and there would be no sense of *al-Walaa' wa'l-Baraa'* (loyalty and friendship towards Muslims, disavowal and enmity towards *kuffar*), or *jihad* and fighting to make the word of Allah supreme in the earth of Allah.

"Fight against those who (1) believe not in Allah, (2) nor in the Last Day, (3) nor forbid that which has been forbidden by Allah and His Messenger (Muhammad((4) and those who acknowledge not the religion of truth (i.e. Islâm) among the people of the Scripture (Jews and Christians), until they pay the *Jizyah* with willing submission, and feel themselves subdued." [*al-Tawbah* 9:29]

"and fight against the *Mushrikoon* (polytheists, pagans, idolaters, disbelievers in the Oneness of Allah) collectively as they fight against you collectively. But know that Allah is with those who are *Al-Muttaqoon* (the pious)" [*al-Tawbah* 9:36]

"O you who believe! Take not as (your) *Bitaanah* (advisors, consultants, protectors, helpers, friends) those outside your religion (pagans, Jews, Christians, and hypocrites) since they will not fail to do their best to corrupt you. They desire to harm you severely. Hatred has already appeared from their mouths, but what their breasts conceal is far worse. Indeed We have made plain to you the *Ayaat* (proofs, evidences, verses) if you understand." [*Aal 'Imraan* 3:118]

If the call to unite the religions is made by a Muslim, this considered to be blatant apostasy from the religion of Islam, because it conflicts with the basic principles of belief. It is an acceptance of disbelief in Allah and a contradiction of the truth of the Qur'an and its abrogation of all laws and religions that came before it. On this basis, it is an idea that should be rejected from the point of view of sharee'ah, and it is definitely haraam according to the evidence of Islam, Qur'an, *Sunnah* and *ijmaa'* (scholarly consensus).

Based on the above:

It is not permissible for a Muslim who believes in Allah as his Lord, Islam as his religion and Muhammad as his Prophet and Messenger, to call people to this evil idea, to encourage it or to propagate it among the Muslims, let alone respond to it or join the conferences and gatherings held to promote it. It is not permissible for a Muslim to print the *Tawraat* and *Injeel* on their own, so how about printing them with the Qur'an in one volume? Whoever does this or calls for it is far astray, because by doing so he is combining truth (the Qur'an) with that which is either distorted or was true but has now been abrogated (the *Tawraat* and *Injeel*).

Similarly, it is not permissible for a Muslim to respond to the call to build a mosque, church and synagogue in one place, because this involves recognizing a religion in which Allah is worshipped other than Islam, and rejecting the idea that Islam should prevail over all other religions, and giving the idea that there are three religions and that it is OK for people to belong to any of these three. This is a kind of equality which implies that Islam does not abrogate the religions that came before it. Undoubtedly, if a person approves of this, believes it or accepts it, this is kufr and misguidance, because it clearly goes against the Qur'an, the *Sunnah* and the consensus (*ijmaa*') of the Muslims and implies that the distortions of the Jews and Christians come from Allah −exalted be He far above that. By the same token, it is not permitted to call churches "Houses of God" or to say that the people there are worshipping Allah in a correct and acceptable manner, because this worship is not done according to the religion of Islam, On the contrary, they are houses in which disbelief (*kufr*) in Allah is expressed; we seek refuge with Allah from *kufr* and its people. Shaykh al-Islam Ibn Taymiyah (may Allah have mercy on him) said in *Majmoo' al-Fataawaa* (22/162): "They — churches and syna-gogues — are not houses of Allah; the houses of Allah are the mosques. On the contrary, they are houses in which disbelief (*kufr*) in Allah is expressed. Even if Allah is mentioned therein, houses are the same as the people in them, and the people in these houses are *kuffar*, so they are the houses of worship of the *kuffar*."

It should be noted that it is obligatory on the Muslims to call the *kuffar* in general, and the People of the Book in particular, to Islam through the clear texts of the Qur'an and *Sunnah*. But this is only to be done by explaining to them and arguing with them in a way that is better (with good words and in a good manner) (cf. *Al-'Ankaboot* 29:46), not by compromising any of the beliefs of laws of Islam. This is in order to convince them about Islam and bring them into the religion, or to establish proof against them so that those who are to be destroyed (for their rejecting the Faith) might be destroyed after a clear evidence, and those who are to live (i.e. believers) might live after a clear evidence.

> "Say (O Muhammad): "O people of the Scripture (Jews and Christians): Come to a word that is just between us and you, that we worship none but Allah (Alone), and that we associate no partners with Him, and that none of us shall take others as lords besides Allah. Then, if they turn away, say: "Bear witness that we are Muslims." [Aal 'Imraan 3:64]

The Committee has made the above statement to the people. We advise the Muslims in general, and people of knowledge in particular, to fear Allah and be aware that He is always watching, to guard Islam and to protect the 'aqeedah (belief) of the Muslims from misguidance and those who promote it and from kufr and its people, and to beware of this idea.

Sheikh Muhammad Salih Al-Munajjid
http://www.islamqa.com/index.php?ref=10213&ln=eng&txt

Question : I have been advised by several Muslims who are knowledgeable in Islam against living in a *kafir* country (America). I am an American/Arab who has lived in America all my life but for a few months now was living in Arabic country, however things are getting hard for me to continue living here (lack of income, housing etc) and am considering going back to America, also another strong reason is that the Health care system is better and free for my wife who is ill. Please give me as much a detailed answer from the *Hadith* and Quran as you can as I don't know for

sure if I should strive to continue living here or go back to America regarding Islam.

Answer: The basic principle is that it is *haraam* to settle among the *mushrikeen* and in their land. If Allah makes it easy for a person to move from such a country to a Muslim country, then he should not prefer that which is inferior [i.e., living in a non-Muslim country] to that which is better [living in a Muslim country] unless he has an excuse which permits him to go back.

We advise you, as others have, not to go and live in a *kafir* country, unless you are forced to go there temporarily, such as seeking medical treatment that is not readily available in a Muslim country.

Note that whoever gives up a thing for the sake of Allah, Allah will compensate him with something better, and that with hardship comes ease, and that whosoever fears Allah and keeps his duty to Him, He will make a way for him to get out (from every difficulty), and He will provide him from (sources) he never could imagine. You should also note that preserving one's capital is better than taking a risk in the hope of making a profit; the Muslim's capital is his religion, and he should not risk it for the sake of some transient worldly gain.

Shaykh Ibn 'Uthaymeen (may Allah have mercy on him) issued a detailed *fatwa* concerning the issue of settling in a *kafir* country, which we will quote here.

Shaykh Ibn 'Uthaymeen said: Settling in a *kafir* country poses a great danger to the Muslim's religious commitment, morals, behavior and etiquette. We and others have seen how many of those who settled there went astray and came back different from when they went; they have come back as evildoers, and some have come back having apostatized from their religion and disbelieving in it and in all other religions — we seek refuge with Allah — denying it completely and mocking the religion and its people, past and present. Hence we must take measures to guard against that and stipulate conditions which will prevent people from following this path which leads to doom and destruction.

There are two basic conditions which must be met before staying in *kafir* countries:

The first condition is: that the person must be secure in his religious commitment, so that he has enough knowledge, faith and willpower to ensure that he will adhere firmly to his religion and beware of deviating or going astray, and that he has an attitude of enmity and hatred of the *kuffar* and will not befriend them and love them, for befriending them and loving them are things that contradict faith. Allah says (interpretation of the meaning): "You (O Muhammad) will not find any people who believe in Allah and the Lasy Day, making friendship with those who oppose Allah and His Messenger (Muhammad), even though they were their fathers or their sons or their brothers or their kindred (people)." [*al-Mujaadilah* 58:22]

And He says: "O you who believe! Take not the Jews and the Christians as *Awliyaa'* (friends, protectors, helpers), they are but *Awliyaa'* of each other. And if any amongst you takes them (as *Awliyaa'*), then surely, he is one of them. Verily, Allah guides not those people who are the *Zaalimoon* (polytheists and wrongdoers and unjust). And you see those in whose hearts there is a disease (of hypocrisy), they hurry to their friendship, saying: 'We fear lest some misfortune of a disaster may befall us.' Perhaps Allah may bring a victory or a decision according to His Will. Then they will become regretful for what they have been keeping as a secret in themselves." [*al-Maah'idah* 5:51,51]

And it was narrated in *al-Saheeh* that the Prophet said: "Whoever loves a people is one of them" and that "A man will be with the one whom he loves."

Loving the enemies of Allah is one of the most serious dangers for the Muslim, because loving them implies that one agrees with them and follows them, or at the very least that one does not denounce them, hence the Prophet (peace and blessings of Allah be upon him) said, "Whoever loves a people is one of them."

The second condition is that he should be able to practice his religion openly, so that he can observe the rituals of Islam with no impediment. So he will not be prevented from establishing regular prayer, and praying *Jumu'ah* and offering prayers in congregation if there are others there with whom he can pray in congregation and pray *Jumu'ah*; and he will not be prevented from paying *zakaah*, fasting, performing *Hajj* and doing other rituals of Islam. If he will not be able to do that then it is not permissible to stay there because it becomes obligatory to migrate (*hijrah*) in that case.

Shaykh Ibn 'Uthaymeen said — explaining the categories of people who settle in non- Muslim lands:

The fourth category includes those who stay for an individual, permissible need, such as doing business or receiving medical treatment. It is permissible for them to stay as long as they need to. The scholar (may Allah have mercy on them) have stated that it is permissible to go to *kafir* countries in order to do business, and they narrated that some of the *Sahaabah* (may Allah be pleased with them) had done that.

The Shaykh said [at the end of the *fatwa*]: How can the believer be content to live in the land of the *kuffar* where the rituals of *kufr* are proclaimed openly and rule belongs to someone other than Allah and His Messenger, seeing that with his own eyes, hearing that with his own ears and approving of it, and even starting to feel that he belongs there and living there with his wife and children, and feeling as comfortable there as he does in the Muslim lands, even though he and his wife and children are in such great danger and their religious commitment and morals are in such peril?

Majmoo' Fataawa al-Shaykh Ibn 'Uthyameen,
http://www.islam-qa.com/index.php?ref=27211&ln=eng

Question : There are people who claim that the *kuffar* love the Muslims, and that their intentions towards us are good. What is your opinion about what they say?

Answer: The enmity of the *kuffar* — the People of the Book (Jews and Christians), *mushrikeen* (polytheists) and hypocrites — towards the believers will last until the Hour begins. The conflict between truth and falsehood will continue until Allah inherits the earth and whomsoever is upon it. Allah says (interpretation of the meaning): "And they will never cease fighting you until they turn you back from your religion (Islamic Monotheism) if they can. And whosoever of you turns back from his religion and dies as a disbeliever, then his deeds will be lost in this life and in the Hereafter, and they will be the dwellers of the Fire. They will abide therein forever" [al-Baqarah 2:17]

Because Islam rules the believers with justice, and gives each person his rights, and they do not want this to happen — for this reason they strive to wage war against this religion and to refute the truth with falsehood. But they can never achieve that, for this religion will abide, and Allah will perfect His light, even though the *kafiroon* hate that.

The *kuffar* want all the nations of this earth to follow kufr as one: "They wish that you reject Faith, as they have rejected (Faith), and thus that you all become equal (like one another) [al-Nisaa' 4:89]

Allah has told us how strong the enmity of the *kuffar* is towards the Muslims:

> "Neither those who disbelieve among the people of the Scripture (Jews and Christians) nor *Al-Mushrikoon* (the idolaters, polytheists, disbelievers in the Oneness of Allah, pagans) like that there should be sent down unto you any good from your Lord. But Allah chooses for His Mercy whom He wills. And Allah is the Owner of Great Bounty." [al-Baqarah 2:105]

No matter what the *kuffar* do, their enmity will not end. Even though they may speak words of friendship, their hearts are filled with hatred towards Islam and its people:

> "How (can there be such a covenant with them)
> that when you are overpowered by them, they regard
> not the ties, either of kinship or of covenant with

you? With (good words from) their mouths they please you, but their hearts are averse to you, and most of them are *Faasiqoon* (rebellious, disobedient to Allah.)" [*al-Tawbah* 9:8]

The People of the Book disbelieve in the verses of Allah, and mix truth with falsehood. They conceal the truth and plot against Islam, in order to divert the Muslims from their religion.

All of the *kuffar*, be they the People of the Book (Jews and Christians), *mushrikeen* (polytheists) or hypocrites, are the enemies of the Muslims, so it is not permissible to depend upon them or to rely on them.

Allah says: "Let not the believers take the disbelievers as *Awliyaa'* (supporters, helpers) instead of the believers, and whoever does that, will never be helped by Allah in any way, except if you indeed fear a danger from them. And Allah warns you against Himself (His punishment), and to Allah is the final return." [*Aal 'Imraan* 3:28]

Allah has warned us against taking the Jews and Christians as friends, and He told us that whoever takes them as friends is one of them. "O you who believe! Take not the Jews and the Christians as *Awliyaa'* (friends, protectors, helpers), they are but Awliyaa' of each other. And if any amongst you takes them (as Awliyaa'), then surely, he is one of them. Verily, Allah guides not those people who are the *Zaalimoon* (polytheists and wrongdoers and unjust)." [*al-Maaidah* 5:51]

All of the *kuffar*, be they the People of the Book (Jews and Christians) *mushrikeen* (polytheists) or hypocrites, will be in Hell on the Day of Resurrection.

"Verily, those who disbelieve (in the religion of Islam, the Qur'an and Prophet Muhammad) from among the people of the Scripture (Jews and Christians) and *Al-Mushrikoon* will abide in the fire of Hell. They are the worst of creatures" [*al-Bayyinah* 98:6] The *kuffar* and the Jews are the greediest of mankind for life, because they know that they have no share in the Hereafter. They hate death because they fear what comes after it, as Allah tells us about the Jews and *mushrikeen* "And verily, you will find them (the Jews) the greediest of mankind for life and (Even greedier) than those who ascribe partners to Allah (and do not believe in Resurrection — Magians, pagans, and idolaters). Everyone of them wishes that he could be given a life of a thousand years. But the grant of such life will not save him even a little from (due) punishment. And Allah is All-Seer of what they do." [*al-Baqarah* 2:96]

From Usool al-Deen al-Islami by Shaykh Muhammad ibn Ibraaheem al-Tuwayjri

http://www.islam-qa.com/index.php?ref=11400&ln=eng&txt

Question : Can a Muslim celebrate a non-Muslim holiday like Thanksgiving?

Answer: Greeting the *kuffar* on Christmas and other religious holidays of theirs is (sinful and forbidden) *haraam*.

http://www.islam-qa.com/index.php?ref=947&ln=eng&txt=??????

Question : What is the ruling on eating the food (rice, meat, chicken or cake) that is given to us by a Christian friend that he made for his birthday or for Christmas or the Christian New Year? What is your opinion on congratulating him by saying, "Insha Allah you will continue to do well this year" so as to avoid saying *Kull 'aam wa antum bi khayr* (approx. "season's greetings") or "Happy New Year," etc?

Answer: It is not permissible for a Muslim to eat things that the Jews and Christians make on their festivals, or what they give him as a gift on their festivals, because that is cooperating with them and joining in with them in this evil.

It is not permissible for him to congratulate them on their festivals in any way whatsoever, because that implies approval of their festival and not denouncing them, and helping them to manifest their symbols and propagate their innovation, and sharing their happiness during their festivals, which are innovated festivals that are connected to false beliefs that are not approved of in Islam.

http://www.islam-qa.com/index.php?ref=81977&ln=eng&txt

Question : I have some questions about Islam, could you explain them for me? What does Islam say about people of other religions? Are all non-Muslim people regarded as sinners because they do not follow Allah and Islam? Can any non-Muslim person enter Paradise without following Islam?

Answer: The ruling of Islam concerning other religions is that they are all either fabricated and false, or abrogated.

The fabricated and false religions are those like the ancient Arabian practice of worshipping idols and stones.

The abrogated religions are those which were taught by the Prophets who came before our Prophet Muhammad. They are valid in that their origins are from Allah, but Islam came and took their place, not with regard to basic beliefs such as the existence of God, the angels, Paradise and Hell, for these are matters which all the Messengers have in common, but there are differences between them with regard to ways of worshipping and drawing close to Allah by means of prayer, fasting, pilgrimage, alms, etc. The later followers of the Prophets have fallen into deviations of belief and shirk, but Islam came to point that out and bring people back to the correct belief taught by the earlier Prophets.

The evidence for that is the verse in which Allah says "And whoever seeks a religion other than Islam, it will never be accepted of him, and in the Hereafter he will be one of the losers." [*Aal 'Imraan* 3:85]

Islam does not regard them (followers of other religions) only as sinners, but as *kuffar* (disbelievers) who will abide forever in the Fire of Hell, as stated in the verse quoted above.

He (the *kafir*) will be a loser in Hell, and will not come of out it. It is not possible for a *kafir* to enter Paradise unless he becomes Muslim.

http://www.islam-qa.com/index.php?ref=21534&ln=eng

Question : What are the actions which, if a Muslim does them, he will be an apostate from Islam?

Answer: Note that Allah has commanded all people to enter Islam and to adhere to it and to beware of whatever is contrary to it. He sent His Prophet Muhammad (peace and blessings of Allah be upon him) to call mankind to that. He tells us that those who follow him will be guided and that those who turn away from him have gone astray. In many verses He warns against the means that lead to apostasy and all forms of *shirk* and *kufr*. The scholars (may Allah have mercy on them) have said, when discussing apostasy, that a Muslim may apostatize from his religion by doing many acts that nullify Islam, which makes it permissible to shed his blood and seize his wealth, and which will put him beyond the pale of Islam. Among the most serious and most common of these things are ten which were mentioned by Shaykh Muhammad ibn 'Abd al-Wahhaab and other scholars (may Allah have mercy on them all). We will mention them in brief here, so that you and others can beware of them, in the hope that you will be safe and sound. We will also explain a little about them after mentioning each one.

Shirk or associating others in worship with Allah. Allah says (interpretation of the meaning): "Verily, Allah forgives not (the sin of) setting up partners (in worship) with Him, but He forgives whom He wills, sins other than that, and whoever sets up partners in worship with Allah, has indeed strayed far away." [*al-Nisa'* 4:116]

"Verily, whosoever sets up partners (in worship) with Allah, then Allah has forbidden Paradise to him, and the Fire will be his abode." [*al-Maa'idah* 5:72]

That includes praying to the dead, seeking their help, making vows and offering sacrifices to them or to the jinn or to the grave. Whoever sets up intermediaries between himself and Allah, asks them to intercede, and puts his trust in them, is a *kafir* according to scholarly consensus.

Whoever does not regard the *mushrikeen* as *kuffar*, or doubts that they are *kuffar*, or regards their way as correct, is a *kafir*.

Whoever believes that anything other than the teaching of the Prophet (peace and blessings of Allah be upon him) is more complete than his teachings, or that the rulings of anyone else are better than his rulings — such as those who prefer the rule of false laws to his rulings — is a *kafir*.

Whoever hates any part of that which the Prophet (peace and blessings of Allah be upon him) brought, even if he acts in accordance with it, is a *kafir*, because Allah says (interpretation of the meaning): "That is because they hate that which Allah has sent down (this Qur'an and Islamic laws); so He has made their deeds fruitless." [*Muhammad* 47:9]

Whoever makes fun of anything in the religion of the Prophet (peace and blessings of Allah be upon him), or makes fun of any texts that refer to rewards or punishments, is a *kafir*. The evidence for that is the verse (interpretation of the meaning): "Say: Was it at Allah, and His *Ayaat* (proofs, evidences, verses, lessons, signs, revelations, etc.) and His Messenger that you were mocking? Make no excuse; you disbelieved after you had believed." [*al-Tawbah* 9:65-66]

Sihr (witchcraft) — including spells to turn one person against another or to make someone love another. Whoever does this or approves of it is a *kafir*. The evidence for that is the verse (interpretation of the meaning): "but neither of these two (angels) taught anyone (such things) till they had said, 'We are for trial, so disbelieve not (by learning this magic from us.)'" [*al-Baqarah* 2:102]

Supporting the *mushrikeen* and helping them against the Muslims. The evidence for that is the verse in which Allah says (interpretation of the meaning): "O you who believe! Take not the Jews and the Christians as *Awliyaa'* (friends, protectors, helpers), they are but *Awliyaa'* of each other. And if any amongst you takes them (as *Awliyaa'*), then surely, he is one of them. Verily, Allah guides not those people who are the *Zaalimoon* (polytheists and wrongdoers and unjust)." [*al-Maa'idah* 5:51]

Whoever believes that some people are allowed to operate outside the law of Muhammad (peace and blessings of Allah be upon him) just as *al-Khidr* operated outside the law of Moosa (peace be upon him) is a *kafir*, because Allah says (interpretation of the meaning): "And whoever seeks a religion other than Islam, it will never be accepted of him, and in the Hereafter he will be one of the losers." [*Aal 'Imraan* 3:85]

Turning away from the religion of Allah, not learning it and not acting in accordance with it. The evidence for that is the verse (interpretation of the meaning): "And who does more wrong than he who is reminded of the *Ayaat* (proofs, evidences, verses, lessons, signs, revelations, etc.) of his Lord, then turns aside therefrom? Verily, We shall exact retribution from the *Mujrimoon* (criminals, disbelievers, polytheists, sinners)." [*al-Sajdah* 32:22]

With regard to all of these acts that nullify Islam, it makes no difference whether a person is joking, serious or afraid, unless he is forced to do it. All of them are very serious, and they all happen a great deal. The Muslim should beware of them and fear falling into them. We seek refuge with Allah from the things that may incur His wrath and painful punishment. May Allah send blessings and peace upon the best of His creation, Muhammad, and upon his family and companions.

The fourth category includes those who believe that the systems and laws devised by men are better than the sharee'ah of Islam, or equal to it; or that it is permissible to refer to them for judgments and rulings, even if he believes that referring to sharee'ah is better; or that the

Islamic system is not fit to be applied in the twentieth century; or that it was the cause of the Muslims' backwardness; or that it should be limited to a person's relationship with his Lord and not have anything to do with the other affairs of life.

The fourth category also includes those who think that carrying out the ruling of Allah by cutting off the hand of the thief or stoning the married adulterer is not appropriate in the modern age.

That also includes: everyone who believes that it is permissible to rule according to something other than the laws of Allah with regard to interactions, hudood punishments or other matters, even if he does not believe that that is better than the ruling of *sharee'ah*, because by doing so he is regarding as permissible something that Allah has forbidden according to consensus, and everyone who regards as permissible something that Allah has forbidden and is well known to be forbidden in Islam, such that no Muslim has any excuse for not knowing that it is forbidden, such as adultery, alcohol and riba, and ruling by something other than the *sharee'ah* of Allah, is a *kafir* according to the consensus of the Muslims.

http://www.islam-qa.com/index.php?ln=eng&ds=qa&lv=browse&QR=31807&dgn=3

APPENDIX C:
A Common Word between Us and You

A Common Word between Us and You
(Summary and Abridgement)

The text is reproduced here without explanatory notes.

The full text, including the names of the 138 signatories can be downloaded in PDF format from:

http://www.acommonword.com/index.php?lang=en&page=downloads

Translations are available in Arabic, French, Italian, German, Indonesian and Spanish (introduction only).

A Common Word between Us and You
(Summary and Abridgement)

Muslims and Christians together make up well over half of the world's population. Without peace and justice between these two religious communities, there can be no meaningful peace in the world. The future of the world depends on peace between Muslims and Christians.

The basis for this peace and understanding already exists. It is part of the very foundational principles of both faiths: love of the One God, and love of the neighbor. These principles are found over and over again in the sacred texts of Islam and Christianity. The Unity of God, the necessity of love for Him, and the necessity of love of the neighbor is thus the common ground between Islam and Christianity. The following are only a few examples:

Of God's Unity, God says in the Holy Qur'an: Say: He is God, the One!/God, the Self-Sufficient Besought of all! (*Al-Ikhlas*, 112:1–2). Of the necessity of love for God, God says in the Holy Qur'an: So invoke the Name of thy Lord and devote thyself to Him with a complete devotion (*Al-Muzzammil*, 73:8). Of the necessity of love for the neighbor, the Prophet Muhammad r said: "None of you has faith until you love for your neighbor what you love for yourself."

In the New Testament, Jesus Christ u said: 'Hear, O Israel, the Lord our God, the Lord is One./And you shall love the Lord your God with all your heart, with all your soul, with all your mind, and with all your strength.' This is the first commandment./And the second, like it, is this: 'You shall love your neighbor as yourself.' There is no other commandment greater than these." (Mark 12:29–31)

In the Holy Qur'an, God Most High enjoins Muslims to issue the following call to Christians (and Jews — the People of the Scripture):

Say: O People of the Scripture! Come to a common word between us and you: that we shall worship none but God, and that we shall ascribe no partner unto Him, and that none of us shall take others for lords beside God. And if they turn away, then say: Bear witness that we are they who have surrendered (unto Him). (*Aal 'Imran* 3:64)

The words: *we shall ascribe no partner unto Him* relate to the Unity of God, and the words: worship none but God, relate to being totally devoted to God. Hence they all relate to the First and Greatest Commandment. According to one of the oldest and most authoritative commentaries on the Holy Qur'an, the words: that none of us shall take others for lords beside God, mean 'that none of us should obey the other in disobedience to what God has commanded.' This relates to the Second Commandment because justice and freedom of religion are a crucial part of love of the neighbor.

Thus in obedience to the Holy Qur'an, we as Muslims invite Christians to come together with us on the basis of what is common to us, which is also what is most essential to our faith and practice: the Two Commandments of love.

In the Name of God, the Compassionate, the Merciful,

And may peace and blessings be upon the Prophet Muhammad

A Common Word between Us and You

In the Name of God, the Compassionate, the Merciful,

> **Call unto the way of thy Lord with wisdom and fair exhortation, and contend with them in the fairest way. Lo! thy Lord is Best Aware of him who strayeth from His way, and He is Best Aware of those who go aright. (The Holy Qur'an, *Al-Nahl*, 16:125)**

(I) Love of God

Love of God in Islam
The Testimonies of Faith

The central creed of Islam consists of the two testimonies of faith or *Shahadahsi*, which state that: There is no god but God, Muhammad is the messenger of God. These Two Testimonies are the *sine qua non* of Islam. He or she who testifies to them is a Muslim; he or she who denies them is not a Muslim. Moreover, the Prophet Muhammad r said: The best remembrance is: 'There is no god but God'....

The Best that All the Prophets have Said

Expanding on the best remembrance, the Prophet Muhammad r also said: The best that I have said — myself, and the prophets that came before me — is: 'There is no god but God, He Alone, He hath no associate, His is the sovereignty and His is the praise and He hath power over all things.' The phrases which follow the First Testimony of faith are all from the Holy Qur'an; each describe a mode of love of God, and devotion to Him.

The words: *He Alone*, remind Muslims that their hearts must be devoted to God Alone, since God says in the Holy Qur'an: God hath not assigned unto any man two hearts within his body (*Al-Ahzab*, 33:4). God is Absolute and therefore devotion to Him must be totally sincere.

The words: *He hath no associate*, remind Muslims that they must love God uniquely, without rivals within their souls, since God says in the Holy Qur'an: Yet there are men who take rivals unto God: they love them as they should love God. But those of faith are more intense in their love for God.... (*Al-Baqarah*, 2:165). Indeed, [T]heir flesh and their hearts soften unto the remembrance of God.... (*Al-Zumar*, 39:23).

The words: *His is the sovereignty*, remind Muslims that their minds or their understandings must be totally devoted to God, for the sovereignty is precisely everything in creation or existence and everything that the mind can know. And all is in God's Hand, since God says in the Holy Qur'an: Blessed is He in Whose Hand is the sovereignty, and, He is Able to do all things. (*Al-Mulk*, 67:1)

The words: His is the praise remind Muslims that they must be grateful to God and trust Him with all their sentiments and emotions. God says in the Holy Qur'an:

> And if thou wert to ask them: Who created the
> heavens and the earth, and constrained the sun and the
> moon (to their appointed work)? they would say:

God. How then are they turned away? / God maketh the provision wide for whom He will of His servants, and straiteneth it for whom (He will). Lo! God is Aware of all things. / And if thou wert to ask them: Who causeth water to come down from the sky, and therewith reviveth the earth after its death? They verily would say: God. Say: Praise be to God! But most of them have no sense. (*Al-ʿAnkabut*, 29:61–63)

For all these bounties and more, human beings must always be truly grateful:

God is He Who created the heavens and the earth, and causeth water to descend from the sky, thereby producing fruits as food for you, and maketh the ships to be of service unto you, that they may run upon the sea at His command, and hath made of service unto you the rivers; / And maketh the sun and the moon, constant in their courses, to be of service unto you, and hath made of service unto you the night and the day. / And He giveth you of all ye ask of

Him, and if ye would count the graces of God ye cannot reckon them. Lo! man is verily a wrong-doer, an ingrate. (*Ibrahim*, 14:32–34)

Indeed, the *Fatihah* — which is the greatest chapter in the Holy Qur'an — starts with praise to God:

In the Name of God, the Infinitely Good, the All-Merciful. /

Praise be to God, the Lord of the worlds. /

The Infinitely Good, the All-Merciful. /

Owner of the Day of Judgment. /

Thee we worship, and Thee we ask for help. /

Guide us upon the straight path. /

The path of those on whom is Thy Grace, not those

who deserve anger nor those who are astray. (*Al-Fati-hah*, 1:1–7)

The *Fatihah*, recited at least seventeen times daily by Muslims in the canonical prayers, reminds us of the praise and gratitude due to God for His Attributes of Infinite Goodness and All-Mercifulness, not merely for His Goodness and Mercy to us in this life but ultimately, on the Day of Judgement when it matters the most and when we hope to be forgiven for our sins. It thus ends with prayers for grace and guidance, so that we might attain — through what begins with praise and gratitude — salvation and love, for God says in the Holy Qur'an: Lo! those who believe and do good works, the Infinitely Good will appoint for them love. (*Maryam*, 19:96)

The words: *and He hath power over all things*, remind Muslims that they must be mindful of God's Omnipotence and thus fear Godix. God says in the Holy Qur'an: ...[A]nd fear God, and know that God is with the Godfearing. / Spend your wealth for the cause of God, and be not cast by your own hands to ruin; and do good. Lo! God loveth the virtuous. / .... (*Al-Baqarah*, 2:194-5)...

[A]nd fear God, and know that God is severe in punishment. (*Al-Baqarah*, 2:196)

Through fear of God, the actions, might and strength of Muslims should be totally devoted to God. God says in the Holy Qur'an:

> ...[A]nd know that God is with those who fear Him. (*Al-Tawbah*, 9:36)....

> O ye who believe! What aileth you that when it is said unto you: Go forth in the way of God, ye are bowed down to the ground with heaviness. Take ye pleasure in the life of the world rather than in the Hereafter ? The comfort of the life of the world is but little in the Hereafter. / If ye go not forth He will afflict you with a painful doom, and will choose instead of you a folk other than you. Ye cannot harm Him at all. God is Able to do all things. (*Al-Tawbah*, 9:38-39)

The words: His is the sovereignty and His is the praise and He hath power over all things, when taken all together, remind Muslims that just as everything in creation glorifies God, everything that is in their souls must be devoted to God:

> All that is in the heavens and all that is in the earth glorifieth God; His is the sovereignty and His is the praise and He hath power over all things. (*Al-Taghabun*, 64:1)

For indeed, all that is in people's souls is known, and accountable, to God:

> He knoweth all that is in the heavens and the earth, and He knoweth what ye conceal and what ye publish. And God is Aware of what is in the breasts (of men). (*Al-Taghabun*, 64:4)

As we can see from all the passages quoted above, souls are depicted in the Holy Qur'an as having three main faculties: the mind or the intelligence, which is made for comprehending the truth; the will which is made for freedom of choice, and sentiment which is made for loving the good and the beautiful. Put in another way, we could say that man's soul knows through understanding the truth, through willing the good, and through virtuous emotions and feeling love for God. Continuing in the same chapter of the Holy Qur'an (as that quoted above), God orders people to fear Him as much as possible, and to listen (and thus to understand the truth); to obey (and thus to will the good), and to spend (and thus to exercise love and virtue), which, He says, is better for our souls. By engaging everything in our souls — the faculties of knowledge, will, and love — we may come to be purified and attain ultimate success:

> So fear God as best ye can, and listen, and obey, and spend; that is better for your souls. And those who are saved from the pettiness of their own souls, such are the successful.
>
> (*Al-Taghabun*, 64:16)

In summary then, when the entire phrase *He Alone, He hath no associate, His is the sovereignty and His is the praise and He hath power over all things* is added to the testimony of faith — *There is no god but God* — it reminds Muslims that their hearts, their individual souls and all the faculties and powers of their souls (or simply their entire hearts and souls) must be totally devoted and attached to God. Thus God says to the Prophet Muhammad r in the Holy Qur'an:

> Say: Lo! my worship and my sacrifice and my living and my dying are for God, Lord of the Worlds. / He hath no partner. This am I commanded, and I am first of those who surrender (unto Him). / Say: Shall I seek another than God for Lord, when He is Lord of all things? Each soul earneth only on its own account, nor doth any laden bear another's load.... (*Al-An'am*, 6:162-164)

These verses epitomize the Prophet Muhammad's r complete and utter devotion to God. Thus in the Holy Qur'an God enjoins Muslims who truly love God to follow this example, in order in turn to be loved by God:

> Say, (O Muhammad, to mankind): If ye love God, follow me; God will love you and forgive you your sins. God is Forgiving, Merciful. (*Aal 'Imran*, 3:31)

Love of God in Islam is thus part of complete and total devotion to God; it is not a mere fleeting, partial emotion. As seen above, God commands in the Holy Qur'an: *Say: Lo! my worship and my sacrifice and my living and my dying are for God, Lord of the Worlds. / He hath no partner.* The call to be totally devoted and attached to God heart and soul, far from being a call for a mere emotion or for a mood, is in fact an injunction requiring all-embracing, constant and active love of God. It demands a love in which the innermost spiritual heart and the whole of the soul — with its intelligence, will and feeling — participate through devotion.

None Comes with Anything Better

We have seen how the blessed phrase: There is no god but God, He Alone, He hath no associate, His is the sovereignty and His is the praise and He hath power over all things — which is the best that all the prophets have said — makes explicit what is implicit in the best remembrance (There is no god but God) by showing what it requires and entails, by way of devotion. It remains to be said that this blessed formula is also in itself a sacred invocation — a kind of extension of the First Testimony of faith (There is no god but God) — the ritual repetition of which can bring about, through God's grace, some of the devotional attitudes it demands, namely, loving and being devoted to God with all one's heart, all one's soul, all one's mind, all one's will or strength, and all one's sentiment. Hence the Prophet Muhammad r commended this remembrance by saying:

> He who says: 'There is no god but God, He Alone, He hath no associate, His is the sovereignty and His is the praise and He hath power over all things' one hundred times in a day, it is for them equal to setting ten slaves free, and one hundred good deeds are written for them and one hundred bad deeds are effaced, and it is for them a protection from the devil for that day until the evening. And none offers anything better than that, save one who does more than that.

In other words, the blessed remembrance, There is no god but God, He Alone, He hath no associate, His is the sovereignty and His is the praise and He hath power over all things, not only requires and implies that Muslims must be totally devoted to God and love Him with their whole hearts and their whole souls and all that is in them, but provides a way, like its beginning (the testimony of faith) — through its frequent repetition — for them to realize this love with everything they are.

God says in one of the very first revelations in the Holy Qur'an: So invoke the Name of thy Lord and devote thyself to Him with a complete devotion (*Al-Muzzammil*, 73:8).

Love of God as the first and greatest commandment in the Bible

The *Shema* in the Book of Deuteronomy (6:4–5), a centrepiece of the Old Testament and of Jewish liturgy, says: Hear, O Israel: The LORD our God, the LORD is one! / You shall love the LORD your God with all your heart, and with all your soul, and with all your strength.

Likewise, in the New Testament, when Jesus Christ, the Messiah u, is asked about the Greatest Commandment, he answers u:

> But when the Pharisees heard that he had silenced the Sadducees, they gathered together. / Then one of them, a lawyer, asked Him a question, testing Him, and saying, / "Teacher, which is the great commandment in the law?" / Jesus said to him, " 'You shall love the LORD your God with all your heart, with all your soul, and with all your mind.' / This is the first and greatest commandment. / And the second is like it: 'You shall love your neighbor as yourself.' / On these two commandments hang all the Law and the Prophets." (Matthew 22:34–40)

And also:

> Then one of the scribes came, and having heard them reasoning together, perceiving that he had answered them well, asked him, "Which is the first commandment of all?" / Jesus answered him, "The first of all the commandments is: 'Hear, O Israel, the LORD our God, the LORD is one. / And you shall love the LORD your God with all your heart, with all your soul, with all your mind, and with all your strength.' This is the first commandment. / And the second, like it, is this: 'You shall love your neighbor as yourself.' There is no other commandment greater than these." (Mark 12:28–31)

The commandment to love God fully is thus the First and Greatest Commandment of the Bible. Indeed, it is to be found in a number of other places throughout the Bible including: Deuteronomy 4:29, 10:12, 11:13 (also part of the *Shema*), 13:3, 26:16, 30:2, 30:6, 30:10; Joshua 22:5; Mark 12:32–33 and Luke 10:27–28.

However, in various places throughout the Bible, it occurs in slightly different forms and versions. For instance, in Matthew 22:37 (You shall love the LORD your God with all your heart, with all your soul, and with all your mind), the Greek word for "heart" is *kardia*, the word for "soul" is *psyche*, and the word for "mind" is *dianoia*. In the version from Mark 12:30 (And you shall love the LORD your God with all your heart, with all your soul, with all your mind, and with all your strength) the word "strength" is added to the aforementioned three, translating the Greek word *ischus*.

The words of the lawyer in Luke 10:27 (which are confirmed by Jesus Christ u in Luke 10:28) contain the same four terms as Mark 12:30. The words of the scribe in Mark 12:32 (which are approved of by Jesus Christ u in Mark 12:34) contain the three terms *kardia* ("heart"), *dianoia* ("mind"), and *ischus* ("strength.")

In the *Shema* of Deuteronomy 6:4–5 (Hear, O Israel: The LORD our God, the LORD is one! / You shall love the LORD your God with all your heart, and with all your soul, and with all your strength). In Hebrew the word for "heart" is *lev*, the word for "soul" is *nefesh*, and the word for "strength" is *me'od*.

In Joshua 22:5, the Israelites are commanded by Joshua u to love God and be devoted to Him as follows:

> "But take careful heed to do the commandment and the law which Moses the servant of the LORD commanded you, to love the LORD your God, to walk in all His ways, to keep His commandments, to hold fast to Him, and to serve Him with all your heart and with all your soul." (Joshua 22:5)

What all these versions thus have in common — despite the language differences between the Hebrew Old Testament, the original words of Jesus Christ u in Aramaic, and the actual transmitted Greek of the New Testament — is the command to love God fully with one's heart and soul and to be fully devoted to Him. This is the First and Greatest Commandment for human beings.

In the light of what we have seen to be necessarily implied and evoked by the Prophet Muhammad's r blessed saying: 'The best that I have said — myself, and the prophets that came before me — is: 'There is no god but God, He Alone, He hath no associate, His is the sovereignty and His is the praise and He hath power over all things,' we can now perhaps understand the words 'The best that I have said — myself, and the prophets that came before me' as equating the blessed formula 'There is no god but God, He Alone, He hath no associate, His is the sovereignty and His is the praise and He hath power over all things' precisely with the 'First and Greatest Commandment' to love God, with all one's heart and soul, as found in various places in the Bible. That is to say, in other words, that the Prophet Muhammad r was perhaps, through inspiration, restating and alluding to the Bible's First Commandment. God knows best, but certainly we have seen their effective similarity in meaning. Moreover, we also do know (as can be seen in the endnotes), that both formulas have another remarkable parallel: the way they arise in a number of slightly differing versions and forms in different contexts, all of which, nevertheless, emphasize the primacy of total love and devotion to God.

(II) Love of the neighbor

Love of the neighbor in Islam

There are numerous injunctions in Islam about the necessity and paramount importance of love for — and mercy towards — the neighbor. Love of the neighbor is an essential and integral part of faith in God and love of God because in Islam without love of the neighbor there is no true faith in God and no righteousness. The Prophet

Muhammad r said: "None of you has faith until you love for your brother what you love for yourself."And: "None of you has faith until you love for your neighbor what you love for yourself."

However, empathy and sympathy for the neighbor — and even formal prayers — are not enough. They must be accompanied by generosity and self-sacrifice. God says in the Holy Qur'an:

> It is not righteousness that ye turn your faces to the East and the West; but righteous is he who believeth in God and the Last Day and the angels and the Scripture and the prophets; and giveth wealth, for love of Him, to kinsfolk and to orphans and the needy and the wayfarer and to those who ask, and to set slaves free; and observeth proper worship and payeth the poor-due. And those who keep their treaty when they make one, and the patient in tribulation and adversity and time of stress. Such are they who are sincere. Such are the pious. (*Al-Baqarah* 2:177)

And also:

> Ye will not attain unto righteousness until ye expend of that which ye love. And whatsoever ye expend, God is Aware thereof. (*Aal 'Imran*, 3:92)

Without giving the neighbor what we ourselves love, we do not truly love God or the neighbor.

Love of the neighbor in the Bible

We have already cited the words of the Messiah, Jesus Christ u, about the paramount importance, second only to the love of God, of the love of the neighbor:

> This is the first and greatest commandment. / And the second is like it: 'You shall love your neighbor as yourself.' / On these two commandments hang all the Law and the Prophets. (Matthew 22:38–40)

And:

> And the second, like it, is this: 'You shall love your neighbor as yourself.' There is no other commandment greater than these." (Mark 12:31)

It remains only to be noted that this commandment is also to be found in the Old Testament:

> You shall not hate your brother in your heart. You shall surely rebuke your neighbor, and not bear sin because of him. / You shall not take vengeance, nor bear any grudge against the children of your people, but you shall love your neighbor as yourself: I am the LORD. (Leviticus 19:17–18)

Thus the Second Commandment, like the First Commandment, demands generosity and self-sacrifice, and On these two commandments hang all the Law and the Prophets.

(III) Come to a common word between us and you

A Common Word

Whilst Islam and Christianity are obviously different religions — and whilst there is no minimising some of their formal differences — it is clear that the Two Greatest Commandments are an area of common ground and a link between the Qur'an, the Torah and the New Testament. What prefaces the Two Commandments in the Torah and the New Testament, and what they arise out of, is the Unity of God — that there is only one God. For the Shema in the Torah, starts: (Deuteronomy 6:4) Hear, O Israel: The LORD our God, the LORD is one! Likewise, Jesus u said: (Mark 12:29) "The first of all the commandments is: 'Hear, O Israel, the LORD our God, the LORD is one." Likewise, God says in the Holy Qur'an: Say: He, God, is One. / God, the Self-Sufficient Besought of all. (*Al-Ikhlas*, 112:1–2). Thus the Unity of God, love of Him, and love of the neighbor form a common ground upon which Islam and Christianity (and Judaism) are founded.

This could not be otherwise since Jesus u said: (Matthew 22:40) "On these two commandments hang all the Law and the Prophets." Moreover, God confirms in the Holy Qur'an that the Prophet Muhammad r brought nothing fundamentally or essentially new: Naught is said to thee (Muhammad) but what already was said to the messengers before thee (*Fussilat* 41:43). And: Say (Muhammad): I am no new thing among the messengers (of God), nor know I what will be done with me or with you. I do but follow that which is Revealed to me, and I am but a plain warner (*Al-Ahqaf*, 46:9). Thus also God in the Holy Qur'an confirms that the same eternal truths of the Unity of God, of the necessity for total love and devotion to God (and thus shunning false gods), and of the necessity for love of fellow human beings (and thus justice), underlie all true religion:

And verily We have raised in every nation a messenger, (proclaiming): Worship God and shun false gods. Then some of them (there were) whom God guided, and some of them (there were) upon whom error had just hold. Do but travel in the land and see the nature of the consequence for the deniers! (*Al-Nahl*, 16:36)

> We verily sent Our messengers with clear proofs, and revealed with them the Scripture and the Balance, that mankind may stand forth in justice.... (*Al-Hadid*, 57:25)

Come to a Common Word!

In the Holy Qur'an, God Most High tells Muslims to issue the following call to Christians (and Jews — the People of the Scripture):

> Say: O People of the Scripture! Come to a common word between us and you: that we shall worship none but God, and that we shall ascribe no partner unto Him, and that none of us shall take others for lords beside God. And if they turn away, then say: Bear witness that we are they who have surrendered (unto Him). (*Aal 'Imran* 3:64)

Clearly, the blessed words: we shall ascribe no partner unto Him relate to the Unity of God. Clearly also, worshipping none but God, relates to being totally devoted to God and hence to the First and Greatest Commandment. According to one of the oldest and most authoritative commentaries (*tafsir*) on the Holy Qur'an — the *Jami' Al-Bayan fi Ta'wil Al-Qur'an* of Abu Ja'far Muhammad bin Jarir Al-Tabari (d. 310 A.H. / 923 C.E.) — that none of us shall take others for lords beside God, means 'that none of us should obey in disobedience to what God has commanded, nor glorify them by prostrating to them in the same way as they prostrate to God.' In other words, that Muslims, Christians and Jews should be free to each follow what God commanded them, and not have 'to prostrate before kings and the like'; for God says elsewhere in the Holy Qur'an: Let there be no compulsion in religion.... (*Al-Baqarah*, 2:256). This clearly relates to the Second Commandment and to love of the neighbor of which justice and freedom of religion are a crucial part. God says in the Holy Qur'an:

> God forbiddeth you not those who warred not against you on account of religion and drove you not out from your homes, that ye should show them kindness and deal justly with them. Lo! God loveth the just dealers. (*Al-Mumtahinah*, 60:8)

We thus as Muslims invite Christians to remember Jesus's u words in the Gospel (Mark 12:29–31):

> ...the LORD our God, the LORD is one. / And you shall love the LORD your God with all your heart, with all your soul, with all your mind, and with all your strength.' This is the first commandment. / And the second, like it, is this: 'You shall love your neighbor as yourself.' There is no other commandment greater than these.

As Muslims, we say to Christians that we are not against them and that Islam is not against them — so long as they do not wage war against Muslims on account of their religion, oppress them and drive them out of their homes, (in accordance with the verse of the Holy Qur'an [*Al-Mumtahinah*, 60:8] quoted above). Moreover, God says in the Holy Qur'an:

> They are not all alike. Of the People of the Scripture there is a staunch community who recite the revelations of God in the night season, falling prostrate (before Him). / They believe in God and the Last Day, and enjoin right conduct and forbid indecency, and vie one with another in good works. These are of the righteous. / And whatever good they do, nothing will be rejected of them. God is Aware of those who ward off (evil). (*Aal-'Imran*, 3:113-115)

Is Christianity necessarily against Muslims? In the Gospel Jesus Christ u says:

> He who is not with me is against me, and he who does not gather with me scatters abroad. (Matthew 12:30)

> For he who is not against us is on our side. (Mark 9:40)

> ...for he who is not against us is on our side. (Luke 9:50)

According to the Blessed Theophylact's Explanation of the New Testament, these statements are not contradictions because the first statement (in the actual Greek text of the New Testament) refers to demons, whereas the second and third statements refer to people who recognised Jesus, but were not Christians. Muslims recognize Jesus Christ as the Messiah, not in the same way Christians do (but Christians themselves anyway have never all agreed with each other on Jesus Christ's u nature), but in the following way... the Messiah Jesus son of Mary is a Messenger of God and His Word which he cast unto Mary and a Spirit from Him... (*Al-Nisa,'* 4:171). We therefore invite Christians to consider Muslims not against and thus with them, in accordance with Jesus Christ's u words here.

Finally, as Muslims, and in obedience to the Holy Qur'an, we ask Christians to come together with us on the common essentials of our two religions... that we shall worship none but God, and that we shall ascribe no partner unto Him, and that none of us shall take others for lords beside God... (*Aal 'Imran*, 3:64).

Let this common ground be the basis of all future interfaith dialogue between us, for our common ground is that on which hangs all the Law and the Prophets (Matthew 22:40). God says in the Holy Qur'an:

> Say (O Muslims): We believe in God and that which is revealed unto us and that which was revealed unto Abraham, and Ishmael, and Isaac, and Jacob, and the tribes, and that which Moses and Jesus received, and that which the prophets received from their Lord. We make no distinction between any of them, and unto Him we have surrendered. / And if they believe in the like of that which ye believe, then are they rightly guided. But if they turn away, then are they in schism, and God will suffice thee against them. He is the Hearer, the Knower. (*Al-Baqarah*, 2:136-137)

Between Us and You

Finding common ground between Muslims and Christians is not simply a matter for polite ecumenical dialogue between selected religious leaders. Christianity and Islam are the largest and second largest religions in the world and in history. Christians and Muslims reportedly make up over a third and over a fifth of humanity respectively. Together they make up more than 55% of the world's population, making the relationship between these two religious communities the most important factor in contributing to meaningful peace around the world. If Muslims and Christians are not at peace, the world cannot be at peace. With the terrible weaponry of the modern world; with Muslims and Christians intertwined everywhere as never before, no side can unilaterally win a conflict between more than half of the world's inhabitants. Thus our common future is at stake. The very survival of the world itself is perhaps at stake.

And to those who nevertheless relish conflict and destruction for their own sake or reckon that ultimately they stand to gain through them, we say that our very eternal souls are all also at stake if we fail to sincerely make every effort to make peace and come together in harmony. God says in the Holy Qur'an: Lo! God enjoineth justice and kindness, and giving to kinsfolk, and forbiddeth lewdness and abomination and wickedness. He exhorteth you in order that ye may take heed (*Al Nahl*, 16:90). Jesus Christ u said: Blessed are the peacemakers... (Matthew 5:9), and also: For what profit is it to a man if he gains the whole world and loses his soul? (Matthew 16:26).

So let our differences not cause hatred and strife between us. Let us vie with each other only in righteousness and good works. Let us respect each other, be fair, just and kind to another and live in sincere peace, harmony and mutual goodwill. God says in the Holy Qur'an:

> And unto thee have We revealed the Scripture with the truth, confirming whatever Scripture was before it, and a watcher over it. So judge between them by that which God hath revealed, and follow not their desires away from the truth which hath come unto thee. For each We have appointed a law and a way. Had God willed He could have made you one community. But that He may try you by that which He hath given you (He hath made you as ye are). So vie one with another in good works. Unto God ye will all return, and He will then inform you of that wherein ye differ. (*Al-Ma'idah*, 5:48)

Wal-Salaamu 'Alaykum,
Pax Vobiscum.

APPENDIX D:
Loving God and Neighbor Together

Loving God and Neighbor Together

A Christian Response to *A Common Word Between Us and You*

In the name of the Infinitely Good God whom we should love with all our Being

Preamble

As members of the worldwide Christian community, we were deeply encouraged and challenged by the recent historic open letter signed by 138 leading Muslim scholars, clerics, and intellectuals from around the world. *A Common Word Between Us and You* identifies some core common ground between Christianity and Islam which lies at the heart of our respective faiths as well as at the heart of the most ancient Abrahamic faith, Judaism. Jesus Christ's call to love God and neighbor was rooted in the divine revelation to the people of Israel embodied in the Torah (Deuteronomy 6:5; Leviticus 19:18). We receive the open letter as a Muslim hand of conviviality and cooperation extended to Christians worldwide. In this response we extend our own Christian hand in return, so that together with all other human beings we may live in peace and justice as we seek to love God and our neighbors.

Muslims and Christians have not always shaken hands in friendship; their relations have sometimes been tense, even characterized by outright hostility. Since Jesus Christ says, "First take the log out your own eye, and then you will see clearly to take the speck out of your neighbor's eye" (Matthew 7:5), we want to begin by acknowledging that in the past (e.g. in the Crusades) and in the present (e.g. in excesses of the "war on terror") many Christians have been guilty of sinning against our Muslim neighbors. Before we "shake your hand" in responding to your letter, we ask forgiveness of the All-Merciful One and of the Muslim community around the world.

Religious Peace — World Peace

"Muslims and Christians together make up well over half of the world's population. Without peace and justice between these two religious communities, there can be no meaningful peace in the world." We share the sentiment of the Muslim signatories expressed in these opening lines of their open letter. Peaceful relations between Muslims and Christians stand as one of the central challenges of this century, and perhaps of the whole present epoch. Though tensions, conflicts, and even wars in which Christians and Muslims stand against each other are not primarily religious in character, they possess an undeniable religious dimension. If we can achieve religious peace between these two religious communities, peace in the world will clearly be easier to attain. It is therefore no exaggeration to say, as you have in *A Common Word Between Us and You*, that "the future of the world depends on peace between Muslims and Christians."

Common Ground

What is so extraordinary about *A Common Word Between Us and You* is not that its signatories recognize the critical character of the present moment in relations between Muslims and Christians. It is rather a deep insight and courage with which they have identified the common ground between the Muslim and Christian religious communities. What is common between us lies not in something marginal nor in something merely important to each. It lies, rather, in something absolutely central to both: love of God and love of neighbor. Surprisingly for many Christians, your letter considers the dual command of love to be the foundational principle not just of the Christian faith, but of Islam as well. That so much common ground exists — common ground in some of the fundamentals of faith — gives hope that undeniable differences and even the very real external pressures that bear down upon us can not overshadow the common ground upon which we stand together. That this common ground consists in love of God and ofneighbor gives hope that deep cooperation between us can be a hallmark of the relations between our two communities.

Love of God

We applaud that A Common Word Between Us and You stresses so insistently the unique devotion to one God, indeed the love of God, as the primary duty of every believer. God alone rightly commands our ultimate allegiance. When anyone or anything besides God commands our ultimate allegiance — a ruler, a nation, economic progress, or anything else — we end up serving idols and inevitably get mired in deep and deadly conflicts.

We find it equally heartening that the God whom we should love above all things is described as being Love. In the Muslim tradition, God, "the Lord of the worlds," is "The Infinitely Good and All-Merciful." And the New Testament states clearly that "God is love" (1 John 4:8). Since God's goodness is infinite and not bound by anything, God "makes his sun rise on the evil and the good, and sends rain on the righteous and the unrighteous," according to the words of Jesus Christ recorded in the Gospel (Matthew 5:45).

For Christians, humanity's love of God and God's love of humanity are intimately linked. As we read in the New Testament: "We love because he [God] first loved us" (1 John 4:19). Our love of God springs from and is nourished by God's love for us. It cannot be otherwise, since the Creator who has power over all things is infinitely good.

Love of Neighbor

We find deep affinities with our own Christian faith when *A Common Word Between Us and You* insists that love is the pinnacle of our duties toward our neighbors. "None of you has faith until you love for your neighbor what you love for yourself," the Prophet Muhammad said. In the New Testament we similarly read, "whoever does not love [the neighbor] does not know God" (1 John 4:8) and "whoever does not love his brother whom he has seen cannot love God whom he has not seen" (1 John 4:20). God is love, and our highest calling as human beings is to imitate the One whom we worship.

We applaud when you state that "justice and freedom of religion are a crucial part" of the love of neighbor. When justice is lacking, neither love of God nor love of the neighbor can be present. When freedom to worship God according to one's conscience is curtailed, God is dishonored, the neighbor oppressed, and neither God nor neighbor is loved.

Since Muslims seek to love their Christian neighbors, they are not against them, the document encouragingly states. Instead, Muslims are with them. As Christians we resonate deeply with this sentiment. Our faith teaches that we must be with our neighbors — indeed, that we must act in their favor — even when our neighbors turn out to be our enemies. "But I say unto you," says Jesus Christ, "Love your enemies and pray for those who persecute you, so that you may be children of your Father in heaven; for he makes his sun rise on the evil and on the good" (Matthew 5:44–45). Our love, Jesus Christ says, must imitate the love of the infinitely good Creator; our love must be as unconditional as is God's — extending to brothers, sisters, neighbors, and even enemies. At the end of his life, Jesus Christ himself prayed for his enemies: "Forgive them; for they do not know what they are doing" (Luke 23:34).

The Prophet Muhammad did similarly when he was violently rejected and stoned by the people of Ta'if. He is known to have said, "The most virtuous behavior is to engage those who sever relations, to give to those who withhold from you, and to forgive those who wrong you." (It is perhaps significant that after the Prophet Muhammad was driven out of Ta'if, it was the Christian slave 'Addas who went out to Muhammad, brought him food, kissed him, and embraced him.)

The Task Before Us

"Let this common ground" — the dual common ground of love of God and of neighbor — "be the basis of all future interfaith dialogue between us," your courageous letter urges. Indeed, in the generosity with which the letter is written you embody what you call for. We most heartily agree. Abandoning all "hatred and strife," we must engage in interfaith dialogue as those who seek each other's good, for the one God unceasingly seeks our good. Indeed, together with you we believe that we need to move beyond "a polite ecumenical dialogue between selected religious leaders" and work diligently together to reshape relations between our communities and our nations so that they genuinely reflect our common love for God and for one another.

Given the deep fissures in the relations between Christians and Muslims today, the task before us is daunting. And the stakes are great. The future of the world depends on our ability as Christians and Muslims to live together in peace. If we fail to make every effort to make peace and come together in harmony you correctly remind us that "our eternal souls" are at stake as well.

We are persuaded that our next step should be for our leaders at every level to meet together and begin the earnest work of determining how God would have us fulfill the requirement that we love God and one another. It is with humility and hope that we receive your generous letter, and we commit ourselves to labor together in heart, soul, mind and strength for the objectives you so appropriately propose.

Harold W. Attridge
Dean and Lillian Claus Professor of New Testament, Yale Divinity School

Miroslav Volf
Founder and Director of the Yale Center for Faith and Culture, Henry B. Wright Professor of Theology, Yale University

Joseph Cumming
Director of the Reconciliation Program, Yale Center for Faith and Culture

Emilie M. Townes
Andrew Mellon Professor of African American Religion and Theology and President-elect of the American Academy of Religion

SIGNATORIES

A selection of prominent signatories follows. These signatories consist of those featured in the November 18, 2007 *New York Times* publication of *Loving God and Neighbor Together*, as well as of a selection of other prominent signatories. These signatories were all confirmed via email and in most cases were reconfirmed by further email exchange.

Capt. Bradford E. Ableson, Chaplain Corps, US Navy and Senior Episcopal Chaplain in the US Navy

Dr. Martin Accad, Academic Dean, Arab Baptist Theological Seminary (Lebanon), Director, Institute of Middle East Studies (Lebanon), Associate Professor of Islamic Studies, Fuller School of Intercultural Studies

Scott C. Alexander, Associate Professor of Islam and Director, Catholic-Muslim Studies, Catholic Theological Union

Dr. Mogamat-Ali Behardien, Minister, African Reformed Church, Paarl, South Africa.

Roger Allen, Professor of Arabic and Comparative Literature and Chair, Department of Near Eastern Languages and Civilizations, University of Pennsylvania, member of Middle East Study Group of the Episcopal Diocese of Pennsylvania

Jean Amore, CSJ, for the Leadership Team of the Sisters of St. Joseph, Brentwood, NY

Leith Anderson, President, National Association of Evangelicals

Rev. Daniel S. Appleyard, Rector, Christ Episcopal Church, Dearborn, MI

William Aramony, Consultant

Harold W. Attridge, Dean and Lillian Claus Professor of New Testament, Yale Divinity School

Dr. Don Argue, Chancellor, Northwest University, Former President, National Association of Evangelicals, Commissioner, United States Commission on International Religious Freedom

David Augsburger, Professor of Pastoral Care and Counseling, Fuller Theological Seminary

Gerald R. Baer, M.D., Minister of Christian Education, Landisville, PA

Dwight P. Baker, Associate Director, Overseas Ministries Study Center

Dr. Ray Bakke, Convening Chair, Evangelicals for Middle East Understanding: An International Coalition, Tempe, AZ

His Lordship Bishop Camillo Ballin, MCCI, Vicar Apostolic of Kuwait

Leonard Bartlotti, Associate Professor of Intercultural Studies, Biola University

Charles L. Bartow, Carl and Helen Egner Professor of Speech Communication in Ministry, Princeton Theological Seminary

Rt. Rev. Barry Beisner, Bishop, Episcopal Diocese of Northern California

Federico Bertuzzi, President, PM Internacional, Latin America

James A. Beverley, Professor of Christian Thought and Ethics, Tyndale Seminary, Toronto, Canada

J.D. Bindenagel, former U.S. Ambassador and Vice President, DePaul University, Chicago, IL

Rev. Dr. Thomas W. Blair, The Second Presbyterian Church of Baltimore

Walter R. Bodine, Pastor, International Church at Yale and Research Affiliate, Near Eastern Languages, Yale University

Rev. Timothy A. Boggs, St. Alban's Episcopal Church, Washington, DC

Regina A. Boisclair, Cardinal Newman Chair of Theology, Alaska Pacific University, Anchorage, Alaska

David Bok, Independent Bible Teacher, Hartford Seminary, Hartford, CT

Rev. Jim Bonewald, Pastor, Knox Presbyterian Church, Cedar Rapids, IA

Jonathan J. Bonk, Executive Director, Overseas Ministries Study Center and Editor, International Bulletin of Missionary Research

Rev. Michael S. Bos, Director, Al Amana Centre, Sultanate of Oman

Steven Bouma-Prediger, Professor of Religion, Hope College, Holland, MI

Gerhard Böwering, Professor of Religious Studies, Yale University

Mary C. Boys, Skinner and McAlpin Professor of Practical Theology, Union Theological Seminary, New York, NY

Dan Brannen, International Students, Inc.

Revs. Scott & Katarina Breslin, Protestant House Church Network, Istanbul Turkey

Rev. Dr. Stuart Briscoe, Minister at Large, Elmbrook Church, Brookfield Wisconsin, USA; Founder, "Telling the Truth, Inc."

Rev. Douglas Brown, Pastor, Valley View United Methodist Church Overland Park, Kansas

Joseph Britton, Dean, Berkeley Divinity School at Yale

Huib Bruinink, Developer of Marketing, PT. Puteri Mawar Sari, Central Java, Indonesia

John M. Buchanan, Editor/Publisher, The Christian Century.

James J. Buckley, Dean, College of Arts and Sciences, Loyola College in Maryland

Eugene W. Bunkowske, Ph.D., Fiechtner Chair Professor of Christian Outreach, Oswald Huffman School of Christian Outreach, Concordia University, St. Paul, Minnesota

John R. Burkholder, Professor Emeritus, Religion and Peace Studies, Goshen College, Goshen, IN

David Burkum, Pastor, Valley Christian Church, Lakeville, MN

Rt. Rev. Joe Goodwin Burnett, Bishop, Episcopal Diocese of Nebraska

Allen Busenitz, International Student Ministry, West Lafayette, IN

Very Rev. Samuel G. Candler, Dean, Cathedral of St. Philip (Anglican), Atlanta, GA

Juan Carlos Cárdenas, Academic Director, Instituto Iberoamericano de Estudios Transculturales, Granada, Spain

Joseph Castleberry, President, Northwest University

Rev. Colin Chapman, Former Lecturer in Islamic Studies, Near East School of Theology, Beirut, Lebanon, and author of Whose Promised Land?

Ellen T. Charry, Assoc. Professor of Systematic Theology, Princeton Theological Seminary

David Yonggi Cho, Founder and Senior Pastor of Yoido Full Gospel Church, Seoul, Korea

Hyung Kyun Chung, Associate Professor of Ecumenical Studies, Union Theological Seminary in New York

Rev. Richard Cizik, Vice President of Governmental Affairs, National Association of Evangelicals

Rev. Dr. Emmanuel Clapsis, Professor of Systematic Theology, Holy Cross Greek Orthodox School of Theology, Brookline, MA

William Clarkson IV, President, The Westminster Schools, Atlanta, Georgia

Emily Click, Lecturer on Ministry and Assistant Dean for Ministry Studies and Field Education, Harvard Divinity School.

Corneliu Constantineanu, Dean and Associate Professor of New Testament, Evangelical Theological Seminary, Osijek, Croatia

Robert E. Cooley, President Emeritus, Gordon-Conwell Theological Seminary, South Hamilton, Massachusetts

Rev. Shawn Coons, St. Philip Presbyterian, Houston, TX

Harvey Cox, Hollis Professor of Divinity, Harvard Divinity School

Joseph Cumming, Director of the Reconciliation Program, Yale Center for Faith and Culture, Yale Divinity School

Daniel A. Cunningham, Executive Pastor, Temple Bible Church, Temple, TX

Bryant L. Cureton, President, Elmhurst College, Elmhurst, IL

Fr. John D'Alton, President, Melbourne Institute for Orthodox Christian Studies, Melbourne, Australia

Fr. Joseph P. Daoust, S.J., President, Jesuit School of Theology at Berkeley, CA

Rev. David R. Davis, Special Projects Coordinator, The Evangelical Alliance Mission, Wheaton, IL

John Deacon, Leader, Branch Out Ministries, The Olive Branch Community Church, Markham, Ontario, Canada

Rev. Joseph C. Delahunt, Senior Pastor, Silliman Memorial Baptist Church, Bridgeport, CT

André Delbecq, Thomas J. and Kathleen L. McCarthy University Professor, Center for Spirituality of Organizational Leadership and former Dean of the Leavey School of Business at the University of Santa Clara

Dr. John Dendiu, Assistant Professor of Religion, Bethel College (Indiana)

David A. Depew, President, Seed of Abraham Association, Broadcasting radio Bible studies in the Middle East

Keith DeRose, Allison Foundation Professor of Philosophy, Yale University

Curtiss Paul DeYoung, Professor of Reconciliation Studies, Bethel University

Andrew Dimmock, Director, Doulos Community, Nouakchott, Mauritania

Chip Dobbs-Allsopp, Associate Professor of Old Testament, Princeton Theological Seminary

Linda Tempesta Ducrot, President, Chez Ducrot, Inc., Plymouth, MA

Andrés Alonso Duncan, CEO, Latinoamerica Global, A.C.

Kent A. Eaton, Professor of Pastoral Ministry and Associate Dean, Bethel Seminary San Diego, California

Diana L. Eck, Professor of Comparative Religion and Indian Studies in Arts and Sciences and member of the Faculty of Divinity, Harvard University

Mike Edens, Professor of Theology and Islamic Studies, Associate Dean of Graduate Studies, New Orleans Baptist Theological Seminary, New Orleans, LA

Mark U. Edwards, Jr., Senior Advisor to the Dean, Harvard Divinity School

James Ehrman, Director, Global Ministries Office, Evangelical Congregational Church

Bertil Ekstrom, Executive Director, Mission Commission, World Evangelical Alliance

Nancie Erhard, Assistant Professor of Comparative Religious Ethics, Saint Mary's University, Halifax, Nova Scotia

John Esposito, University Professor & Founding Director Prince Alwaleed Bin

Talal Center for Muslim-Christian Understanding, Georgetown University

Chester E. Falby, Priest Associate, St. Catherine's Episcopal Church, Manzanita, OR

Thomas P. Finger, Mennonite Central Committee, Evanston, IL

Rev. Dr. David C. Fisher, Senior Minister, Plymouth Church, Brooklyn, NY

David Ford, Regius Professor of Divinity, Cambridge University

Marlene Malahoo Forte, 2007 Yale World Fellow, Fuller Theological Seminary, Pasadena, CA

Rev. Susan L. Gabbard, St. John's United Church of Christ, Mifflinburg, PA

Millard Garrett, Vice President, Eastern Mennonite Missions, Salunga, PA

Siobhan Garrigan, Assistant Professor of Liturgical Studies and Assistant Dean for Marquand Chapel, Yale Divinity School

Timothy George, Dean, Beeson Divinity School, Samford University

William Goettler, Assistant Dean for Assessment and Ministerial Studies, Yale Divinity School

Michael J. Goggin, Chairperson, North American Interfaith Network (NAIN)

Robert S. Goizueta, Professor of Theology, Boston College

Bruce Gordon, Professor of History, University of St. Andrews

William A. Graham, Albertson Professor of Middle Eastern Studies in Arts and Sciences and O'Brian Professor of Divinity and Dean in the Divinity School, Harvard University

Wesley Granberg-Michaelson, general secretary, Reformed Church in America

Rev. Bruce Green, Bridge Building Facilitator, FCM Foundation, Centerville Presbyterian Church, Fremont, CA

Joel B. Green, Professor of New Testament Interpretation, Fuller Theological Seminary

Lynn Green, International Chairman, Youth With A Mission

Frank Griffel, Associate Professor of Islamic Studies, Yale University

Rev. Giorgio Grlj, Pastor, Rijeka Baptist Church, Baptist Union of Croatia

Rev. Kent Claussen Gubrud, Christus Victor Lutheran Church, Apple Valley, MN

Rt. Rev. Edwin F. Gulick, Jr., Bishop, Episcopal Diocese of Kentucky

Judith Gundry-Volf, Adjunct Associate Professor of New Testament, Yale Divinity School

David P. Gushee, Distinguished Professor of Christian Ethics, McAfee School of Theology at Mercer University and President, Evangelicals for Human Rights

Kim B. Gustafson, President, Common Ground Consultants, Inc.

Elie Haddad, Provost, Arab Baptist Theological Seminary, Lebanon

Dr. Anette Hagan, Elder, Mayfield Salisbury Parish Church, Edinburgh, Scotland

Martin Hailer, Professor of Theology, Leuphana University, Lueneburg, Germany

Rev. L. Ann Hallisey, Hallisey Consulting and Counseling, Interim Vicar, Good Shepherd Episcopal Church, Berkeley, CA

Gloria K. Hannas, Member, Peacemaking Mission Team of the Presbytery of Chicago, PCUSA, La Grange, IL

Paul D. Hanson, Florence Corliss Lamont Professor of Divinity, Harvard Divinity School

Pastor Peter Hanson, Director of Studies, Dept. of Theology and Training, Lutheran Church of Senegal

Heidi Hadsell, President, Hartford Seminary, Hartford, CT

David Heim, Executve Editor, The Christian Century

Richard Henderson, Director of Studies, Westbrook Hay, United Kingdom

Mary E. Hess, Associate Professor of Educational Leadership, Luther Seminary

Richard Heyduck, Pastor, First United Methodist Church, Pittsburg, TX

Rev. Dr. David M. Hindman, United Methodist campus minister, The Wesley Foundation at The College of William and Mary, Williamsburg, VA

Rev. Norman A. Hjelm, Director, Commission on Faith and Order (retired), National Council of the Churches of Christ in the USA

Carl R. Holladay, Charles Howard Candler Professor of New Testament, Candler School of Theology, Emory University

Jan Holton, Assistant Professor of Pastoral Care, Yale Divinity School

Marian E. Hostetler, former worker, Mennonite Mission Network and Eastern Mennonite Mission, Elkhart, IN

Joseph Hough, President and William E. Dodge Professor of Social Ethics, Union Theological Seminary in New York

Bill Hybels, Founder and Senior Pastor, Willow Creek Community Church, South Barrington, IL

Dale T. Irvin, President and Professor of World Christianity, New York Theological Seminary, New York, NY

Dr. Nabeel T. Jabbour, Consultant, Professor, Colorado Springs, CO

Todd Jenkins, Pastor, First Presbyterian Church, Fayetteville, TN

David L. Johnston, Lecturer, Religious Studies Department, University of Pennsylvania

Robert K. Johnston, Professor of Theology and Culture, Fuller Theological Seminary

Rt. Rev. Shannon Sherwood Johnston, Bishop Co-adjutor, Episcopal Diocese of Virginia

Rt. Rev. David Colin Jones, Bishop Suffragan, Episcopal Diocese of Virginia

Gary D. Jones, Rector, St. Stephen's Episcopal Church, Richmond, VA

Tony Jones, National Coordinator, Emergent Village

Stefan Jung, Economist, Germany

Rev. Dr. Riad A. Kassis, Theologian, Author, and Consultant

Sister Helen Kearney, Sisters of Saint Joseph, Brentwood, NY

Sister Janet Kinney, CSJ, Sisters of St. Joseph, Brentwood, NY

Doris G. Kinney, associate editor (ret.), Time Inc., New York

Steve Knight, National Coordinating Group Member, Emergent Village, Charlotte, NC

Paul Knitter, Paul Tillich Professor of Theology, World Religions and Culture, Union Theological Seminary in New York

Dr. Manfred W. Kohl, Vice President of Overseas Council International, USA

Rev. John A. Koski, Assemblies of God, Dearborn, MI

Very Rev. Dr. James A. Kowalski, Dean, The Cathedral Church of Saint John the Divine, New York NY

James R. Krabill, Senior Executive for Global Ministries, Mennonite Mission Network, Elkhart, IN

Hank Kraus, Founder and Director, PeaceMark

Sharon Kugler, University Chaplain, Yale University

Catherine Kurtz, Landisville Mennonite Church, Landisville, PA

Peter Kuzmic, Eva B. and Paul E. Toms Distinguished Professor of World Missions and European Studies, Gordon-Conwell Theological Seminary and Rektor, Evandjeoski Teoloski Fakultet, Osijek, Croatia

Jonathan L. Kvanvig, Distinguised Professor of Philosophy, Baylor University

David Lamarre-Vincent, Executive Director, New Hampshire Council of Churches

John A. Lapp, Executive Secretary Emeritus, Mennonite Central Committee, Akron, PA

Dr. Warren Larson, Director of the Zwemer Center for Muslim Studies, Columbia International University, SC

Traugott Lawler, Professor of English emeritus, Yale University

Dr. Maurice Lee, post-doctoral fellow, Harvard University

Rt. Rev. Peter J. Lee, Bishop, Episcopal Diocese of Virginia

Kristen Leslie, Associate Professor of Pastoral Care, Yale Divinity School

Linda LeSourd Lader, President, Renaissance Institute, Charleston, SC

Rev. R. Charles Lewis, Jr., Parish Associate, First Presbyterian-Vintage Faith Church, Santa Cruz, CA

Julyan Lidstone, OM, Glasgow, Scotland

Erik Lincoln, Author of Peace Generation tolerance curriculum for Muslim Students, Indonesia

John Lindner, Director of External Relations, Yale Divinity School

Greg Livingstone, Founder, Frontiers and historian of Muslim-Christian encounter

Albert C. Lobe, Interim Executive Director, Mennonite Central Committee, Akron, PA

Rick Love, International Director, Frontiers and Adjunct Associate Professor of Islamic Studies, Fuller Theological Seminary, author of Peacemaking

Donald Luidens, Professor of Sociology, Hope College, Holland, MI

Owen Lynch, Associate Pastor, Trent Vineyard, Nottingham, UK

Douglas Magnuson, Associate Professor of Intercultural Programs and Director of Muslim Studies, Bethel University

Peter Maiden, International Coordinator, OM

Jozef Majewski, Doctor of Theology, Professor of Media Studies at the University of Gdansk, Poland

Danut Manastireanu, Director for Faith & Development, Middle East & East Europe Region, World Vision International, Iasi, Romania

Rev. Dr. John T. Mathew, Minister, St. Mark's United Church of Canada, & Deptartment of Religious Studies, Huntington/Laurentian Universities, Sudbury, ON Canada

Rev. Steven D. Martin, President, Vital Visions Incorporated and Pastor, United Methodist Church, Oak Ridge, TN

Harold E. Masback, III, Senior Minister, The Congregational Church of New Canaan

Rt. Rev Gerald N. McAllister, Retired Bishop, Episcopal Diocese of Oklahoma

The Rev. Donald M. McCoid, Executive for Ecumenical and Inter-Religious Relations, Evangelical Lutheran Church in America

C. Douglas McConnell, PhD, Dean, School of Intercultural Studies, Fuller Seminary

Sister Mary McConnell, CSJ, Sisters of St. Joseph, Brentwood, NY

Don McCurry, President, Ministries to Muslims

Jeanne McGorry, CSJ, Sisters of St. Joseph, Brentwood, NY

Elsie McKee, Archibald Alexander Professor of Reformation Studies and the History of Worship, Princeton Theological Seminary

Scot McKnight, Karl A. Olsson Professor in Religious Studies, North Park University, Chicago, IL

Brian D. McLaren, Author, Speaker, Activist

C. Edward McVaney, Retired Chairman, CEO and President, J.D. Edwards and Company

Kathleen E. McVey, J. Ross Stevenson Professor of Early and Eastern Church History, Princeton Theological Seminary

Carl Medearis, President, International Initiatives, Denver, CO

Greg Meland, Director of Formation, Supervised Ministry and Placement, Bethel Seminary, Minnesota

Judith Mendelsohn Rood, Ph.D., Associate Professor of History and Middle Eastern Studies, Department of History, Government, and Social Science School of Arts and Sciences, Biola

Mennonite Central Committee, Akron, PA

Harold E. Metzler, Member, Church of the Brethren and heritor of the Amish/Mennonite tradition

Alan E. Miller, Lead Pastor, Conestoga Church of the Brethren, Leola, PA

David B. Miller, Pastor, University Mennonite Church, State College, PA

Rev. Dr. Sid L. Mohn, President, Heartland Alliance for Human Needs and Human Rights, Chicago, IL

Brother Benilde Montgomery, O.S.F., Franciscan Brother of Brooklyn

Steve Moore, President & CEO, The Mission Exchange

Douglas Morgan, Director, Adventist Peace Fellowship

Richard Mouw, President and Professor of Christian Philosophy, Fuller Theological Seminary

Salim J. Munayer, Academic Dean, Bethlehem Bible College, Jerusalem

Rich Nathan, Senior Pastor, Vineyard Church of Columbus

David Neff, Editor in Chief & Vice-President, Christianity Today Media Group

Alexander Negrov, President, Saint Petersburg Christian University, St. Petersburg, Russia

Arnold Neufeldt-Fast, Associate Dean, Tyndale Seminary, Toronto

Craig Noll, Assistant Editor, International Bulletin of Missionary Research, Overseas Ministries Study Center

Rev. Roy Oksnevad, Institute of Strategic Evangelism at Wheaton College

Dennis Olsen, Charles T. Haley Professor of Old Testament Theology, Princeton Theological Seminary

Richard R. Osmer, Thomas Synnot Professor of Christian Education, Princeton Theological Seminary

Rev. Canon Mark Oxbrow, International Mission Director, Church Mission Society, UK

Rt. Rev. George E. Packard, Bishop Suffragan for Chaplaincies of the Episcopal Church

George Parsenios, Assistant Professor of New Testament, Princeton Theological Seminary

Greg H. Parsons, General Director, USCWM, Pasadena, CA

Stephanie A. Paulsell, Houghton Professor of the Practice of Ministry Studies, Harvard Divinity School

James R. Payton, Jr., Professor of History, Redeemer University College, Ancaster, Ontario, Canada and President, Christians Associated for Relationships with Eastern Europe

Emily A. Peacock, Circuit Judge, 13th Judicial Circuit of Florida, Tampa, Florida

Doug Pennoyer, Dean, School of Intercultural Studies, Biola University

Howard Pepper, M.A., M.Div., President, Nurture Press, San Diego, CA

Douglas Petersen, Margaret S. Smith Professor of Intercultural Studies, Vanguard University of Southern California

Rev. Edward Prevost, Rector, Christ Church, Winnetka, Illinois

Bruce G. Privratsky, Elder, Holston Conference, United Methodist Church

Sally M. Promey, Professor of Religion & Visual Culture, Professor of American Studies, Professor Religious Studies and Deputy Director, Institute of Sacred Music, Yale University

Rev. Erl G. Purnell, Rector, Old Saint Andrew's Episcopal Church, Bloomfield, CT

Rev. John C. Ramey, President, Aslan Child Rescue Ministries and President, The Olive Branch Institute

Robert M. Randolph, Chaplain to the Massachusetts Institute of Technology, Cambridge, MA

Thomas P. Rausch, S.J., T. Marie Chilton Professor of Catholic Theology, Loyola Marymount University, Los Angeles, CA

James D. Redington, S.J., Associate Professor in the Dwan Family Chair of Interreligious Dialogue, Jesuit School of Theology at Berkeley/Graduate Theological Union, CA

David A. Reed, Professor Emeritus of Pastoral Theology and Research, Wycliffe College, Univerity of Toronto, Canada

Neil Rees, International Director, World Horizons

Rev. Warren Reeve, Lead Pastor, Bandung International Church, Bandung, West Java, Indonesia and Founder and Facilitator of the Missional International Church Network

Rodney Allen Reeves, Former moderator of the Christian Church (Disciples of Christ) in Oregon and board member, Greater Portland Institute for Christian-Muslim Understanding and member, Interfaith Council of Greater Portland.

Dr. Evelyne A. Reisacher, Assistant Professor of Islamic Studies and International Relations, Fuller Theological Seminary, Pasadena, CA

Cornel G. Rempel, Retired pastor, chaplain and supervisor of clinical pastoral education, Winnipeg, Manitoba, Canada

Steve Robbins, Pastor and Director, Vineyard Leadership Institute

Cecil M. Robeck, Jr., Professor of Church History and Ecumenics, Fuller Theological Seminary and the Director of the David du Plessis Center for Christian Spirituality

Leonard Rodgers, Executive Director, Evangelicals for Middle East Understanding: An International Coalition, Tempe, AZ

Dudley C. Rose, Lecturer on Ministry and Associate Dean for Ministry Study, Harvard Divinity School

Rev. Herschel Rosser, Associate Pastor, Vineyard Church of Sugar Land, Stafford, TX and Texas Area Church Planting Coordinator, Vineyard, USA

Glenna N. Roukes, Elder, First Presbyterian Church, Santa Cruz, CA and Secretary, Mission Team

Philip Ruge-Jones, Associate Professor of Theology, Texas Lutheran University, Seguin, Texas

William L. Sachs, Director, Center for Reconciliation and Mission, St. Stephen's Episcopal Church, Richmond, Virginia

Robert A. Sain, Pastor, Messiah Lutheran Church, ELCA, Hildebran, NC

Lamin Sanneh, D. Willis James Professor of Missions and World Christianity, Yale University

Andrew D. Saperstein, Associate Director of the Reconciliation Program at the Yale Center for Faith and Culture

Tyler Savage, Missionary with Church Resource Ministries, Germany and South Africa

Meritt Lohr Sawyer, International Program Director, Langham Partnership International

Warren C. Sawyer, President and CEO, The Caleb Foundation, Swampscott, MA

Rev. Dr. Christian Scharen, Director, Faith as a Way of Life Program, Yale Center for Faith & Culture

Rev. Dr. Robert Schuller, Founder, Crystal Cathedral and Hour of Power

Elizabeth Schüssler Fiorenza, Krister Stendahl Professor of Divinity, Harvard Divinity School

Francis Schüssler Fiorenza, Stillman Professor of Roman Catholic Studies, Harvard Divinity School

William Schweiker, Edward L. Ryerson Distinguished Service Professor of Theological Ethics, University of Chicago

Waldron Scott, President emeritus, Holistic Ministries International, Paterson, NJ

Andrew J. Sebanc, Senior Pastor, Green Timbers Covenant Church, Surrey, British Columbia, Canada

Rev. Donald Senior, C.P., President, Catholic Theological Union, Chicago, Illinois

C. L. Seow, Henry Snyder Gehman Professor of OT Language and Literature, Princeton Theological Seminary

Rev. Dr. Perry Shaw, Chair, Faculty of Ministerial Studies, Arab Baptist Theological Seminary, Beirut, Lebanon

Michael T. Shelley, Director, Center of Christian-Muslim Engagement for Peace and Justice, Lutheran School of Theology at Chicago

David W. and K. Grace Shenk, Global Consultants, Eastern Mennonite Missions, Salunga, PA

Wilbert R. Shenk, Senior Professor of Mission History and Contemporary Culture, Fuller Theological Seminary

John N. Sheveland, Assistant Professor of Comparative Theology, Gonzaga University, Washington, DC

Marguerite Shuster, Harold John Ockenga Professor of Preaching and Theology, Fuller Theological Seminary

Frederick J. Sigworth, Professor, Department of Cellular and Molecular Physiology, Yale University

Mark Siljander, Member of the U.S. Congress (r) & fm U.S. Ambassador to the U.N. (atl del)

Walt Simmerman, Pastor, First United Methodist Church, Galax, VA

The Community Council of the Sisters of the Precious Blood, Dayton, OH.

Sister Florence Seifert, CPPS, President; Sister Jeanette Buehler, CPPS, Vice-President; Sister Madonna Ratermann, CPPS, Councilor; Sister Edna Hess, CPPS, Councilor; Sister Marita Beumer, CPPS, Councilor

C. Donald Smedley, Associate Director, The Rivendell Institute, New Haven, CT

John D. Spalding, Founder and Editor, SOMAreview.com

Rev. Andrew Spurr, Vicar of Evesham with Norton and Lenchwick Diocese of Worcester

John G. Stackhouse, Jr., Sangwoo Youtong Chee Professor of Theology and Culture, Regent College, Vancouver, Canada

Glen H. Stassen, Lewis B. Smedes Professor of Chrisian Ethics, Fuller Theological Seminary

Sally Steenland, Senior Policy Advisor, Faith & Progressive Policy Initiative, Center for American Progress, Washington, DC

Wilbur P. Stone, Program Director and Lead Faculty, Global and Contextual Studies, Bethel University/Seminary

Rev. Dr. John Stott, Rector Emeritus, All Souls Church, Langham Place, London, UK

Frederick J. Streets, The Carl and Dorothy Bennett Professor in Pastoral Counseling, The Wurzweiler School of Social Work, Yeshiva University, Adjunct Associate Professor of Pastoral Theology, Yale Divinity School, Former Yale University Chaplain

Diana Swancutt, Associate Professor of New Testament, Yale Divinity School

Merlin Swartz, Professor of Islamic Studies, Boston University

Donald K. Swearer, Director, Center for the Study of World Religions, Harvard Divinity School

Dr. Glen A. Taylor, Cooperative Studies Teaching Fellow, Tajikistan State National University, Dushanbe, Tjikistan

William Taylor, Global Ambassador, World Evangelical Alliance

Harvey Thiessen, Executive Director, OM Canada

Rev. John Thomas, General Minister and President, United Church of Christ

Stephen Thomas, European Team Leader, Salt & Light Ministries Senior Pastor, Oxford, UK

Dr. J. Milburn Thompson, Chair and Professor of Theology, Bellarmine University, Louisville, KY

Iain Torrance, President, Princeton Theological Seminary

Emilie M. Townes, Andrew Mellon Professor of African American Religion and Theology, Yale Divinity School, and President-elect of the American Academy of Religion

Michael W. Treneer, Internation President, The Navigators, Colorado Springs, CO

Geoff Tunnicliffe, International Director, World Evangelical Alliance

Fr. Benjamin J. Urmston, S.J., Director Emeritus Peace and Justice Programs, Xavier University, Cincinnati, OH

Birgit van Hout, Executive Director, Miami Coalition of Christians and Jews (MCCJ), FL

George Verwer, Founder and former International Director, OM

Harold Vogelaar, Director Emeritus: A Center of Christian-Muslim Engagement for Peace and Justice, Lutheran School of Theology at Chicago

Miroslav Volf, Founder and Director of the Yale Center for Faith and Culture, Henry B. Wright Professor of Theology, Yale Divinity School

Fr. H. Eberhard von Waldow, Professor Emeritus, Pittsburgh Theological Seminary

Rev. Berten A. Waggoner, National Director, Association of Vineyard Churches

Robin Wainwright, President, Middle East Fellowship, Pasadena, CA and Chairman of the Executive Committee, Oxford Centre for Mission Studies

Dr. Dale F. Walker, Affiliate Professor, Asbury Theological Seminary, Wilmore, KY

Jim Wallis, President, Sojourners

Charlotte R. Ward, Associate Professor of Physics, Emerita, Auburn University and Life Deacon, Auburn First Baptist Church

Charles H. Warnock III, Senior Pastor, Chatham Baptist Church, Chatham, VA

Rick Warren, Founder and Senior Pastor, Saddleback Church, and The Purpose Driven Life, Lake Forest, CA

Very Rev. Debra Warwick-Sabino, Rector, Grace Episcopal Church, Fairfield, CA

Mark R. Wenger, Director of Pastoral Studies, Lancaster Eastern Mennonite Seminary P.O., Lancaster, PA

Dr. Bob Wenz, Renewing Total Worship Ministries, Colorado Springs, CO

Rev. Laura Westby, Pastor, First Congregational Church of Danbury, CT

Robert R. Wilson, Hoober Professor of Religious Studies, Associate Dean for Academic Affairs, Yale Divinity School

Rev. Michael D. Wilker, Executive Director, Lutheran Volunteer Corps, Washington, DC

Dr. John Wolfersberger, Retired

Breinigsville, PA USA
19 August 2009
222530BV00003B/2/P